HOT SPOTS

HOT SPOTS

WHY SOME TEAMS, WORKPLACES, AND ORGANIZATIONS BUZZ WITH ENERGY—AND OTHERS DON'T

Lynda Gratton

BERRETT-KOEHLER PUBLISHERS, INC.
San Francisco

Berrett-Koehler Publishers, Inc.
235 Montgomery Street, Suite 650
San Francisco, CA 94104-2916
Tel: (415) 288-0260   Fax: (415) 362-2512   www.bkconnection.com

Ordering Information

Quantity sales. Special discounts are available on quantity purchases by corporations, associations, and others. For details, contact the "Special Sales Department" at the Berrett-Koehler address above.

Individual sales. Berrett-Koehler publications are available through most bookstores. They can also be ordered directly from Berrett-Koehler: Tel: (800) 929-2929;
Fax: (802) 864-7626; www.bkconnection.com

Orders for college textbook/course adoption use. Please contact Berrett-Koehler: Tel: (800) 929-2929;
Fax: (802) 864-7626.

Orders by U.S. trade bookstores and wholesalers. Please contact Publishers Group West, 1700 Fourth Street, Berkeley, CA 94710. Tel: (510) 528-1444; Fax (510) 528-3444.

Berrett-Koehler and the BK logo are registered trademarks of Berrett-Koehler Publishers, Inc.

Printed in the United States of America

Berrett-Koehler books are printed on long-lasting acid-free paper. When it is available, we choose paper that has been manufactured by environmentally responsible processes. These may include using trees grown in sustainable forests, incorporating recycled paper, minimizing chlorine in bleaching, or recycling the energy produced at the paper mill.

Library of Congress Cataloging-in-Publication Data

Gratton, Lynda.
  Hot spots : why some teams, workplaces, and organizations buzz with energy—and others don't / by Lynda Gratton.
    p. cm.
   ISBN-13: 978-1-57675-418-4 (hardcover)
  1. Intellectual capital—Management. 2. Organizational behavior—Management. 3. Management—Employee participation. I. Title.

  HD53.G745 2007
  658.4'038—dc22
                          2006023100

First Edition
10 09 08 07 06   10 9 8 7 6 5 4 3 2 1

Interior design and production: Jonathan Peck, Dovetail Publishing Services

*To the memory of my dearest friend Sumantra Ghoshal
—whose wisdom ignites this book.*

Contents

Preface

Many of us spend a good deal of our life working. We make friends at work, we learn about ourselves when we work, we grow and develop, and we become innovative, energized, and stimulated. Working cooperatively with others, we are able to create the positive energy that gives us joy and adds value to our companies. All of these wonderful human experiences can take place during the times we are engaged in work. I call these times Hot Spots. Hot Spots are places and times where cooperation flourishes, creating great energy, innovation, productivity, and excitement. Hot Spots can be workplaces, teams, departments, companies, factories, cities, industries, coffee shops, hallways, conferences—any place or time where people are working together in exceptionally creative and collaborative ways.

Work can be innovating and stimulating; it can also be dreary, predictable, political, and competitive, leaving us drained and exhausted rather than invigorated and excited. In such a state, we are individually and collectively unable to fulfill our own potential or indeed the innovative potential of the companies of which we are members. Rather than the energy and excitement of Hot Spots, we suffer the drain and exhaustion of the Big Freeze.

Why and when are we excited and energized, and what drains this energy from us? Understanding how and why energy at work is created and dissipated has been at the center of my ideas for the past decade. In *Living Strategy: Putting People at the Heart of Corporate Purpose*, I examined the strategic decisions that shape the context that influences engagement and motivation. In *The Democratic Enterprise: Liberating Your Business with Freedom, Flexibility, and Commitment*, I focused on the practices and processes that influence behavior and performance. In a sense, *Hot Spots* completes the trilogy. The underlying values expressed in all three books are similar: the importance of meaning, of humanism, and of the infinite capacity of human potential. In this book, I have shifted the focus from the individual to groups and communities. The key message here is relational, that it is through our relationships with others that our own potential is built and that it is in the relationships between employees that organizational value is created. This marks a renewed interest in what I believe to be some of the most interesting ideas around today: the importance of emergence and the central role communities and networks play in innovation.

In each of these books, my purpose has been to bring the best and most interesting ideas of scholars to executives and to bring the insight and wisdom of executives to students and scholars of business. We have much to learn from each other. I have gained these ideas, insights, and wisdom by working closely with executives, writing case studies about high-performing companies, and conducting research in productive cooperatives.

The research for this book started in 1995 when Sumantra Ghoshal and I studied some of the top-performing companies in the world. I quickly discovered that each company in its own way faced a challenge of creating a context in which Hot Spots could emerge. When I talked with the executives and employees of BP, Goldman Sachs, Nokia, and OgilvyOne, I began to gain a sense of what encourages Hot Spots to emerge. My attention was repeatedly drawn to three elements. In every company, a great deal of executive focus had gone into creating a culture in which people were willing and even eager to cooperate. This willingness to cooperate was crucial to the second element, the capacity of people to work with others outside their boundaries. The third element I found in each of these companies was the capacity to create an igniting purpose, a purpose that converted latent energy into the energy of a Hot Spot. These elements have multiplicative qualities. Each is needed for a Hot Spot, and each multiplies the effect of the others. When I observed Hot Spots over time, I began to see that another rather different element was in play. The initial three elements ensured that the latent energy of the organization was converted and released in Hot Spots; this was crucial. However, for Hot Spots to be productive, a fourth element was needed: the productive capacity of the people in a Hot Spot. This productive capacity reflects the competencies and skills of Hot Spot members to work together, learn about each other, resolve their conflicts, and manage the rhythm and pacing of their work.

The insights from these early studies and the concept of the four elements provided important clues to Hot Spots. To build on these clues, in 2003, my colleagues and I began a large-scale research project on the nature of positive energy and cooperation in groups and their impact on performance, known as the Cooperative Advantage Research. Partnering with executives in seventeen companies, we sent a major research survey to more than five hundred employees in forty-two work teams in the United States, Europe, and Asia. Our interest was in these team members' experience of working, the context in which they worked, the structure of the tasks they performed, and their perceptions of the performance of the team. We also collected data from the leaders and heads of each team and from members of the human resources (HR) function. (A more detailed exploration of the methodology and research process we used can be found in Appendixes B and C.)

The research that supports this book is the result of the efforts and cooperative working of many people. I would like first to acknowledge the Advanced Institute of Management (AIM) for generously supporting the fellowship that made this research and writing possible. Under the founding director, Professor Anne Huff, and the current director, Professor Robin Wensley, the AIM community of scholars became a testing ground for ideas and a place of inspiration and insight. The Cooperative Advantage Research team is a truly extraordinary group of people who have dedicated their time to engaging in one of the most comprehensive studies of cooperative working in large complex companies. So I extend a big thank-you to the research team—Modestas Gelbuda, Janine Nahapiet, Anna-Katrina Neyer, and Andreas Voigt. I would also like to thank Susan Hill for keeping us on track with the survey design over many months and helping us come to grips with the concept of boundary spanners and to thank Hector Rocha for his thoughts and insights about the nature of cooperation. In would also like to thank my research colleagues on the case writing—Alison Donaldson, Susan Hill, Felipe Monteiro, and Michelle Rogan. Thanks also to my assistant at London Business School, Kate Lewis, for working with the many drafts of the book.

My hope was that this would not be simply a piece of academic research, that we could make a real impact on management practice. To do this, I called on my great friend Tammy Erickson, who directs the Concours Institute. For many years, the Concours Group, under the leadership of Ron Christman, has been engaged in building a network of executives and companies that are passionate about learning and sharing. Tammy and I have for over a decade believed that management research must and can address the emerging challenges that executives face.

Tammy Erickson and her team at Concours were indispensable to the research. In particular, I would like to thank Bob Morrison, who steered the research and survey design so that it always met the interests of executives, and Maira Galins, who was the supreme manager when it came to keeping track of the many hundreds of surveys we sent out.

I owe a real debt to the executives who participated in the research. They championed the ideas in their organizations and persuaded and cajoled numerous people to participate in our research. They were enormously helpful in arranging groups and supporting the survey, and many joined the Concours/AIM research group in the London and Boston research workshops. I would like to thank Ricardo Larrabure from ABN AMRO; Hannah McBain from the BBC; Dorian Baroni from BP; June Boyle from BT; Peter Hall from France Telecom; Hope Greenfield from Lehman Brothers; Laura M. Bouvier from Marriott International; Patrick Dailey and Karsten Hetland from Nokia; Jackie Gittins and Tony Jackson from PricewaterhouseCoopers; Stewart Beaumont, John Reid-Dodick, Charles Jennings, and Rich Taylor from Reuters; Donna McNicol from Rogers Communications Group; Greg Aitken from the Royal Bank of Scotland; Johann Nel, Robert Blackburn, and Jürgen Spitzer from Siemens; Drew Watson from Standard Chartered Bank; Pat Nazemetz from Xerox; and John C. Hodge from XL Global Services.

In writing a book about cooperation, it has been a wonderful experience working with Berrett-Koehler, a truly cooperative publishing house. My editors Steve Piersanti and Jeevan Sivasubramaniam, together with the whole community at BK, have developed *Hot Spots* in a way that has delighted me.

My purpose in writing *Hot Spots* is to inspire and to excite. The message has meaning for every one of us—it provides ideas about what we can personally do to ensure that our energy is focused in Hot Spots, as well as insights for executives and HR professionals on how they can shape the context in which Hot Spots can emerge. I believe passionately that work can be a more fulfilling experience and that companies can become more innovative and creative. To do so involves abandoning some old rules we hold dear and embracing new ones. Our lives and the performance of our organizations are infinitely enriched and nourished by Hot Spots. It is in the interests of every one of us to ensure that we are in Hot Spots at least some of the time. And it is in the interests of company leaders to ensure that Hot Spots arise as often as possible.

Lynda Gratton
lgratton@london.edu
www.lyndagratton.com
London Business School

Introduction

ELEMENTS FOR
CREATING HOT SPOTS

Y OU ALWAYS KNOW WHEN you are in a Hot Spot. You feel energized
and vibrantly alive. Your brain is buzzing with ideas, and the people
around you share your joy and excitement. The energy is palpable, bright,
shining. These are times when what you and others have always known
becomes clearer, when adding value becomes more possible. Times when
the ideas and insights from others miraculously combine with your
own in a process of synthesis from which spring novelty, new ideas, and
innovation. Times when you explore together what previously seemed
opaque and distant. We can all remember being in Hot Spots, when
working with other people was never more exciting and exhilarating and
when you knew deep in your heart that what you were jointly achieving
was important and purposeful. On such occasions, time seems to rush by
as you and those around you are "in the flow."[1] Time even seems to stand
still. We enjoy being part of a Hot Spot, and we are healthier, happier
people as a result.[2]

When Hot Spots arise in and between companies, they provide energy
for exploiting and applying knowledge that is already known and genuinely
exploring what was previously unknown. As a consequence, Hot Spots are

marvelous creators of value for organizations and wonderful, life-enhancing phenomena for each of us.

Yet life is not always about being in a Hot Spot, and organizations are not always about generating Hot Spots. How often have you faced a situation when you knew in your heart you could have achieved more? These are times when your energy has drained, when the Big Freeze takes over. There are many times, in many companies, when Hot Spots fail to emerge.

Over 80 percent of the anticipated value from mergers and acquisitions typically fails to materialize. Three out of four joint ventures fall apart after the honeymoon period. Many executives report that they struggle to deliver products to increasingly discerning consumers. Hoped-for innovation never materializes as the marketing function fights with the sales function about internal costing issues.[3] The Big Freeze also has a human toll. An overly competitive working environment where friendships fail to develop is one of the major sources of stress at work and one of the key reasons why talented employees leave a company.

These are very different problems with very similar underlying reasons. As you will see, at the heart of successful mergers and acquisitions, of well-functioning joint ventures, of the launch of global products and the creation of new products are Hot Spots. These are the occasions when we are willing and able to work skillfully and cooperatively within and across the boundaries of the company, when our energy and excitement are inflamed through an igniting question or a vision of the future, times when positive relationships with work colleagues are a real source of deep satisfaction and a key reason why we decide to stay with a company.

For over a decade, my passion has been discovering Hot Spots. From a theoretical perspective, the phenomenon of Hot Spots is complex. As I describe in Appendix B, an understanding of Hot Spots involves at least six disciplines of scholarship, from psychology to economics. Chapter 1 takes an overview of Hot Spots—the elements that support them and the practices that enhance them.

We begin a deeper investigation in Chapter 2 by tracking Hot Spots as they emerge around the world, from Venezuela to China, Singapore to London. Through the experiences of people like Polly and Carlos at BP, Tim and Nigel at OgilvyOne, Pertti and Huang at Nokia, and Amit at Linux, answers to some of the questions about Hot Spots begin to appear. Why and when do Hot Spots emerge? What is it about these people that supported the emergence of Hot Spots, and what role did the leaders of their company play? Why do some Hot Spots flourish while others fail?

The answer can be found in the formula for Hot Spots:

> Hot Spots = (Cooperative Mindset x Boundary Spanning x Igniting Purpose) x Productive Capacity

A cooperative mindset, boundary spanning, and igniting purpose have a multiplicative effect on each other. The lack of any one of these three elements significantly reduces the potential energy of a Hot Spot. The capacity of this potential energy to be translated into productive energy—and hence innovation and value creation—is dependent on the productive capacity of the people within the emerging Hot Spot.

Chapter 3 takes a closer look at how a cooperative mindset emerges. I contend that it is the result of a self-fulfilling cycle in which attitudes drive the design of practices and processes that then legitimize some behaviors and delegitimize others. Emergence of a cooperative mindset depends on leaders' attitudes toward cooperation and competition and their capacity and willingness to craft within the organization a sense of mutuality and collegiality. This first element sets the stage for the emergence of Hot Spots and ensures that the Big Freeze does not take over. However, as the formula shows, the energy of the cooperative mindset has to be channeled across boundaries for the innovative capacity of a Hot Spot to emerge.

Boundary spanning is crucial to the capacity of a Hot Spot to create value through innovation. As you will see, working cooperatively in well-established teams is important for the exchange of knowledge and for understanding what others know. However, the innovation of a Hot Spot arises when new ideas, from people in different groups and communities, are brought together. Crossing boundaries can be tough. There are challenges in working across distances, working with people who are different from us, and working with people who are relative strangers. For Hot Spots to be innovative, this boundary-spanning work is crucial, and Chapter 4 explores how this can be accomplished with ease and elegance.

A mindset of cooperation and the capacity for spanning boundaries creates a deep potential well of latent energy in the organization. People feel a sense of goodwill toward one another, they trust each other, and they are prepared and able to work across boundaries. For this well of latent energy to be released, there has to be a point of ignition. This igniting purpose, as you will see in Chapter 5, can be an igniting vision, question, or task.

Without this flashpoint of ignition, the energy in the potential Hot Spot will dissipate, and its dynamic potential will be lost.

As noted earlier, these three elements have a multiplier effect on each other. Together they are capable of creating energy and excitement. For this energy to be channeled into productive outcomes requires the fourth element, productive capacity. This capacity is the extent to which members within the Hot Spot are capable of working together in a productive manner. As you will see in Chapter 6, this requires skills in meaningful conversation, conflict resolution, and commitment making, together with the capacity of the members of the Hot Spot community to create a rhythm that intersperses periods of pressure with periods of reflection and conversation.

Hot Spots emerge; they cannot be directed or controlled. What then is the role of the leader in Hot Spots? Chapter 7 explores what this role might be. It will be clear from the stories told in Chapter 2 that the leaders of these companies do play a role. However, it is a rather different one from the usual directive and controlling role. It involves supporting conversation, shaping signature practices and processes, and creating networks across which Hot Spots can flourish.

The final chapter takes a closer look at what you can do now in your company to increase the probability of Hot Spots emerging. I suggest five phases of activities, beginning with an examination of the current level of energy within the company and determining where there is potential for Hot Spots to emerge and where the Big Freeze has take over. In Chapter 8, you can begin to build a model of the factors that have resulted in the current situation, together with a deeper understanding of what can be done to change the dynamics of Hot Spots in companies. Appendix A, "Resources for Creating Hot Spots," describes these ways of thinking about the company in a series of diagnostic and profiling tools that you can use with your colleagues and teams.

Much of your life is spent working. My passion over the past two decades has been to visualize and describe a way of working that resonates with our human potential and creates places where value is created. Our experiences of Hot Spots can be exhilarating. This book is an invitation to make this exhilaration part of our everyday experience of work and central to the mission of leaders.

GENERATING EXTRAORDINARY ENERGY

COMPANIES FLOURISH WITH extraordinary energy and fade as energy wanes. The energy in Hot Spots can fuel innovation, which is fast becoming the core capability for organizational success, and ensure that best practices and ideas are incorporated into productivity improvements so that the company remains in the forefront. Hot Spot energy has the potential to trigger new ways of thinking about old problems and of revamping practices and processes to deliver superior services and products. The energy in a Hot Spot can, for example, fuel new ways of thinking about the cost base of a company that bring real insights around cost innovation. The energy of a Hot Spot can even lead us to reinvent the way we think about managing people or the practices that support performance management.

Corporate Thermal Imaging

When extraordinary energy arises, it forms Hot Spots—occasions when people from inside and outside the company are able to engage with each other in a way that they have rarely been able to do. When this energy and the resulting excitement are ignited, they have the power to propel teams to work toward goals they never believed were achievable. Let us examine Hot Spots through the metaphor of thermal imaging.

Imagine for a moment that you are standing on the very peak of a mountain, looking through thermal-imaging goggles that show the extent of energy in the landscape. As you place the goggles over your eyes, you are able to see clearly the vast terrain of valleys and hills spread out in front of you. Imagine that the terrain stretched out before you is the organization.

These particular instruments are sensitive to energy and heat—in this case, the passion of the individual and the energy of the organization. So the terrain you are observing is the terrain of the whole company, and you are seeing people in the company living their day-to-day lives.

As you look through your heat-sensitive goggles, the terrain appears green. Daily work is happening in a predictable way—people are going about their business, and little excitement or energy beyond the norm is being generated. The green signifies "business as usual." As you continue to watch, suddenly, in the distance, you see a flare of bright orange and red erupting. This flare could emerge in many places. It could be a workplace, a particular team or department or factory. It could be in a coffee shop, across a hallway, or in a conference. It could even happen across the whole company. This is a Hot Spot. It is a moment when people are working together in exceptionally creative and collaborative ways. As you watch, other Hot Spots emerge across the terrain. Some of these Hot Spots remain bright red; others fade to orange and then back to green. Then, from the corner of your eye, you see the green in one part of the landscape changing from green to icy blue. The energy in this place, for these people, is beginning to be depleted. As energy depletes, the heat begin to chill, and the Big Freeze has taken over.

Hot Spots occur when the energy within and between people flares—when the mundane of everyday activities is set aside for engaged work that is exciting and challenging. It is at these times that ideas become contagious and new possibilities appear.

As you survey the landscape through your thermal goggles, what do you think causes the changes in energy? Why is it that in some parts of the organization you see the green of the predictable, while in other parts there is the blue of the Big Freeze? And why on occasion does the red of the Hot Spot flare? Are these random occurrences, driven by factors beyond the control of the organization? Are these fluctuations in energy the result of forces that are part of the everyday work of people, forces that are so deep and so complex that they are impossible to predict, let alone control? Should we simply be passive observers of Hot Spots, looking down from the mountain, or are there actions that we can take to increase the probability of Hot Spots emerging?

These are crucial questions for employees who are eager to work in Hot Spots and for executives intent on encouraging the emergence of Hot Spots. My research into this phenomenon shows that the probability of Hot Spots occurring can indeed be increased. There are ways of changing the blue of the Big Freeze to the green of business as usual and even to the red of an innovative Hot Spot. This is good news; however, there is a challenge. The challenge is that to do so, some companies will have to make some rather fundamental changes in the way they are structured, the values they espouse, and the behaviors of executives and leaders.

To see what these changes might entail, let us first take a closer look at what happens in a Hot Spot when it emerges. In companies across the world, I have watched Hot Spots flare. I have seen Hot Spots emerge in the teams that network between Poland and Venezuela in the oil giant BP. I have seen an incredibly innovative Hot Spot emerge in Nokia as teams grapple with ways to serve the Asian market. I have watched in awe as the volunteer programmers in Linux created clusters of Hot Spots that are a formidable competitor to Microsoft and have fundamentally reinvented the way we think about organizations. In each of these companies, I have observed over and over again that a Hot Spot flares through the spontaneous combustion of three elements.

Hot Spots = (Cooperative Mindset x Boundary Spanning x
Igniting Purpose) x Productive Capacity

The First Element: A Cooperative Mindset

One of our most profound insights about Hot Spots is that their innovative capacity arises from the intelligence, insights, and wisdom of people working together. The energy contained in a Hot Spot is essentially a combination of their individual energy with the addition of the relational energy generated between them. In Hot Spots, value is created in the space between people when people come together. As a consequence, the quality and extent of these relationships is crucial to the emergence of Hot Spots, and it is a *cooperative mindset* that is the foundation of these high-quality relationships. Hot Spots arise because people are excited, and willing and able to cooperate with each other. It is these exciting, skillful cooperative relationships that fuel the exchange of knowledge and insights that ignite a Hot Spot and create innovation. Let's take a moment to think about a cooperative mindset and the nature of human potential and human capital.

A key aspect of human potential in Hot Spots is what people know and how they use this knowledge. So in a sense, we can think of a Hot Spot as the sum of all the intellectual capital of the people within it. Although intellectual capital is a crucial aspect of Hot Spots—without it, the Hot Spot becomes dull and tepid—it is not sufficient. The energy flows and ebbs within Hot Spots are just as likely to be caused by emotional capital. This is the emotional insight and ability that people have to adapt and modify their behavior. It is this emotional capital that plays a critical role in self-awareness and self-knowledge. However, the potential energy of a Hot Spot is not simply the addition of the intellectual and emotional capital of all the people who are engaged within it. The effect is a combination effect rather than a simple additive effect. The combination effect occurs as a result of the relationships between people, what we might call the social capital of the Hot Spot. This social capital signifies the depth and extent of relationships within the Hot Spots and the networks of relationships outside the Hot Spot. It is the energy released through these relationships that plays such a crucial role in Hot Spots.

The three aspects combine to form a triangle of human capital and human potential (see Figure 1.1). Hot Spots emerge when all three aspects are engaged in a reinforcing cycle. People become energized and excited about sharing knowledge and about what they might learn from others—their intellectual capital is engaged as they become increasingly emotionally involved. As people feel increasingly passionate about something, they really care, and they enjoy the emotional contagion as others becoming engaged and excited. Hot Spots become extraordinary opportunities for social capital to be created as friendships and relationships are forged and the people involved feel the pleasure of attachment and intimacy.

Where Hot Spots fail, these three aspects of human potential rapidly atrophy. People lose interest, they no longer believe they can learn and develop, and the intellectual challenge is gone. They increasingly withdraw

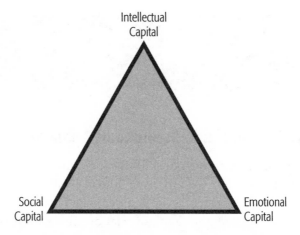

Figure 1.1 The three aspects of human capital and potential

emotionally as the passion of the project wanes and they become increasingly individualistic and uncooperative as relationships cool. Instead of engaging in exciting and skillful cooperation, people become passive or uninterested in each other or even turn competitive and aggressive. Instead of contributing to the learning and innovation of a Hot Spot, they hoard their knowledge and insights, and the level of energy drops to neutral or even disappears entirely. The Big Freeze has taken over.

The emergence of the three elements of human potential begins the process of Hot Spot development. This emergence is in turn dependent on the extent to which individuals value the power of working with others—what I term a cooperative mindset. Without this valuing of cooperation, intellectual and emotional potential are turned inward, to development of the individual, rather than outward, to the development of others and the creation of Hot Spots. Without a deep cooperative mindset, human potential is geared toward producing "superstars" and all the competitive values associated with them. For companies such as Goldman Sachs that actively recruit highly talented people, this emphasis on the cooperative mindset is crucial to ensuring that the firm does not break up into clusters of superstars with their own fiefdoms. Chapter 3 takes a closer look at how companies like Goldman Sachs have created a context in which there is enough of a cooperative mindset that the talents of the firm remain integrated rather than fragmented.

> *Hot Spots = (Cooperative Mindset x Boundary Spanning x*
> *Igniting Purpose) x Productive Capacity*

The Second Element: Boundary Spanning

Within Hot Spots exciting and skillful cooperative relationships thrive, built on the three combined aspects of human capital. These relationships differ in their typology, that is in their depth and extent. This typology is important. The extent and depth of relationships within Hot Spots can have different effects on the business value created within Hot Spots. With regard to the *depth of relationships,* some relationships are strong and have been in place for many years. Other relationships are more of an association or an acquaintance—with people who are known but not known well.

We also found that the *extent of boundary spanning* in the relationships differs within Hot Spots. Some relationships are within the group. Other relationships are with people outside the group, in other functions, or even in other companies. In this case, boundary spanning is high as these networks of relationships cross team, function, and company boundaries.

The effects of these relationships on the capacity of the Hot Spot to create business value is symbolized in Figure 1.2.

The real insight in the first element of a Hot Spot is that a cooperative mindset is crucial to the emergence of a Hot Spot. The insight for the second element is that the nature of the business value created within a Hot Spot differs according to the extent to which boundaries are crossed. Figure 1.2 shows the different ways in which value is created in a Hot Spot. Innovative value is created through *novel combinations* of the ideas, knowledge, and insights of people. Value can also be created as people *exploit their shared expertise* within their group or *explore ideas, knowledge, and insights* with people outside their group. We return to this topic in Chapter 4.

Value creation through exploiting shared expertise

There are times in Hot Spots when the value of the community is created primarily because groups of people have been working together for some time in an activity that has been ignited by a particularly complex or challenging goal. In these circumstances, value within the Hot Spot is created as a result of the members' exploiting and sharing knowledge they already have.

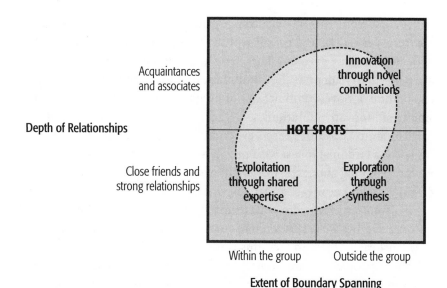

Figure 1.2 Effects of relationship quality on value creation in Hot Spots

This outcome is unlikely to be unusual or innovative because the members of the Hot Spot know each other well and are probably rather similar in their competencies and attitudes. Hence they are unlikely to learn things from one another that they did not already know. As Figure 1.2 illustrates, although Hot Spots can emerge in this lower left quadrant, in reality they need the stimulation of people from outside the group to flourish in the long term.

Value creation through exploration

Some of the relationships within a Hot Spot are strong ones between people who know each other very well but are located in different groups or functions. These strong boundary-spanning relationships are marvelous opportunities for value to be created as each person explores in depth what the other knows.

Value creation through novel combinations

Relationships between people who know each other well and are located in the same group are important for continuous improvement. However, a significant proportion of the cooperative relationships within Hot Spots span to people outside the teams and even outside the boundaries of the company. In Hot Spots, we found marketing people cooperating skillfully with people from sales, people from Poland cooperating skillfully with people from Venezuela, and people within the company cooperating skillfully with customers or partners. These Hot Spots of boundaryless cooperation are particularly adept at the combination of ideas and insights. It is this exploration of novel combinations of insights and ideas that opens the possibility of innovative solutions.

The innovation of these new combinations is most likely to occur under two circumstances: with people who have different mindsets and ways of thinking about the world and with people who are relative strangers rather than know each other very well.

This may at first seem counterintuitive. Surely in Hot Spots, people know each other well and therefore are more able to be cooperative because they trust each other? In fact, this is not the case. Wonderful long friendships with people who are similar are a joy of life. But they are rarely where innovative ideas arise. The reason is simple: much if not most of the knowledge we exchange in these relationships is already known. We are more likely to talk about what we both know, than about what one of us doesn't know. These deep, long-term relationships are an important part of our well-being and are indeed crucial to developing trust and respect in Hot Spots. Hot Spots need both the trust and respect of long-term relationships and the insight and novelty of new relationships that cross boundaries. It is this combination that is most valuable.

If Hot Spots emerge as a result of the relationship between relative strangers with different mindsets, why do they choose to cooperate? This is the alchemy of the Hot Spot. To ignite the energy latent within these relationships, we found the third element—the igniting purpose.

> *Hot Spots = (Cooperative Mindset x Boundary Spanning x*
> *Igniting Purpose) x Productive Capacity*

⚙ The Third Element: Igniting Purpose

Let us return to the metaphor of the thermal goggles. Imagine that you are sitting on the mountain observing the terrain of the company beneath you and the network of cooperative relationships that crisscross the company. These networks of boundaryless cooperative relationships are an essential

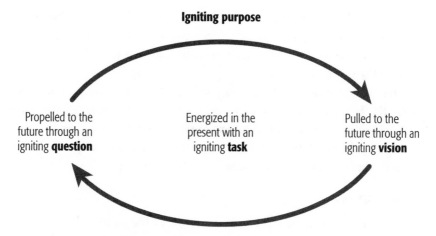

Figure 1.3 Forms an igniting purpose can take

element of Hot Spots. However, often the energy within them remains latent. Through the thermal goggles, the situation looks green—business as usual. As you watch, you see people meeting each other and engaging in good-natured conversations and activities. Yet the energy remains at the green level. These are not Hot Spots. They remain green, with latent energy, because there is nothing igniting them—nothing that captures people's attention and imagination, nothing that they can all collectively get behind, nothing that releases the latent energy.

Thus the flaring of Hot Spots is always accompanied by an *igniting purpose*—something that people find exciting and interesting and worth engaging with. As you will see in Chapter 5, when this igniting purpose occurs, people flock to it—they want to be part of it. As Figure 1.3 illustrates, the igniting purpose can take a number of forms.

Igniting questions

There are occasions when energy is released through the imagination of people being propelled to the future by an *igniting question*. This is a question that is so exciting and stimulating that people immediately wanted to engage with it. As you will see, some igniting questions are big and expansive, like the one BP CEO John Browne asked of his people: "How can we, an oil company, become a force for good?"

People throughout BP leapt to answer this question, engaged by the concept behind it and inspired to innovate. The question triggered "beyond petroleum," the rebranding and repositioning of BP's core business and innovations involving renewable energy sources. These questions create ignition because, like the idea of an oil company as a force for good, they question the dominant logic.

The very idea of an oil company being a force for good seems to go against the grain. That's why questions like Browne's have rarely been asked before. They encapsulate sufficient excitement and intrigue to awaken people's curiosity and intellectual capital and to stimulate the cooperative relationships that crisscross the boundaries of the company.

Igniting visions

Igniting questions invite people to think about the future; the questions essentially propel them into the unknown. However, there is another type of igniting purpose: an *igniting vision*. Rather than propelling people into an unknown future, this purpose creates an image of what the future could be. Here energy is released by creating a context within which people can collectively imagine what it is they are working toward.

At Linux, the extraordinary innovations around building an open source platform that would enable anyone to access it was triggered by a vision Linus Torvalds had as a graduate student at the University of Helsinki. What ignites the energy of the Hot Spots at Linux is that every one of the thousands of people involved has a vision of what it is they are all trying to achieve.

Igniting tasks

For some Hot Spots, the latent energy is released by an *igniting task* that is so interesting, challenging, and potentially developmental that people flock to it spontaneously. At BT, the opportunity to get involved with a task that brought the community and customers into the company was so interesting that over seven hundred people flocked to it. Igniting tasks are intrinsically motivating; people love working on them.

Laying the groundwork

Of course, knowing the formula that produces Hot Spots is not the same as being able to create a Hot Spot. In some companies, there are many Hot Spots blazing, while in others, there are few. Why is this the case? Hot Spots cannot be commanded to appear. Performance controls, orders, and directives make little impact. Hot Spots arise through individual and collective choices, when excitement mounts and curiosity is engaged. Hot Spots cannot be simply summoned forth. However, the ground can be prepared, the elements can be put into place, and the igniting questions can be asked.

The challenge is that many companies have often unwittingly created an environment where competition and self-interest negate a mindset of cooperation. Where "turf wars" destroy the possibilities of working across boundaries. Where dry, tired speech rather than igniting questions is the common parlance, and where a lackadaisical attitude smothers the energy and questioning that might trigger a Hot Spot.

The good news is that much of this can be changed. You can craft a context that favors cooperation rather than competition. You can actively build and support networks of relationships that crisscross the boundaries of the company. You can create the will and the freedom to ask igniting questions. These elements are marvelous creators of energy. However, to focus this energy and ensure that it actually adds value, you need the fourth and final element, productive capacity.

> Hot Spots = (Cooperative Mindset × Boundary Spanning × Igniting Purpose) × <u>Productive Capacity</u>

The Fourth Element: Productive Capacity

Hot Spots that are capable of creating value through innovation are also potentially the most complex. My own research has shown clearly that initially, the most productive teams are those located in the lower left quadrant of Figure 1.2—that is, people who work with each other in the same location and have similar skills and attitudes. Those in the top right corner are potentially the most innovative, but they also tend to be less productive. As you will see in Chapter 6, Hot Spots that remained productive did so because the people in them engaged in what we called *productive practices.* Examples of productive practices are illustrated in Figure 1.4.

In the early phases of productive Hot Spots, there is a real emphasis on working on relationships—appreciating the talents of others, learning to make and keep commitments, and resolving conflicts. As the Hot Spot progresses, the type of productive challenge that members face subtly shifts. Whereas previously it was about the relationships between members, it now

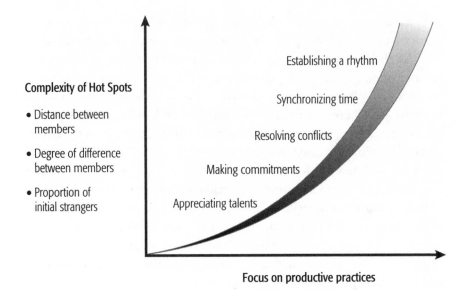

Complexity of Hot Spots

- Distance between members
- Degree of difference between members
- Proportion of initial strangers

Establishing a rhythm

Synchronizing time

Resolving conflicts

Making commitments

Appreciating talents

Focus on productive practices

Figure 1. 4 Complexity and productive practices

shifts to members' attitudes to time and rhythm. Hot Spots whose members fail to make this shift in timing and rhythm burn themselves out as the pace of work accelerates. They also become less creative as their time for reflection is overwhelmed by the growing pace of demands. Without these productive practices, the complexity of Hot Spots can be overwhelming, and the energy in the Hot Spot dissipates.

Designing for the Emergence of Hot Spots

Hot Spots emerge on their own; they cannot be controlled and directed. That does not mean that nothing can be done to encourage their emergence. In fact, there are many ways in which you can actively design for the emergence of Hot Spots. The coming chapters explore four key points of leverage through which Hot Spots can emerge. In particular, as you will see in Chapter 8, Hot Spots can be encouraged through subtle shifts in the structure, practices, and processes of your company and the way that decisions are made and resources are allocated. The probability of Hot Spots emerging can be substantially increased through the way tasks are designed, how feedback is given, and how technology is used to support the Hot Spot community. As you will see in Chapter 7, the skills, role modeling, and competencies of leaders can play a crucial role, as can the motivation and capability of everyone, and in particular the human capacity and attitude toward spanning boundaries.

In companies in which Hot Spots flourish, executives make use of a large portfolio of these points of leverage to unleash the energy and innovation of Hot Spots. Appendix A, "Resources for Creating Hot Spots," provides a host of diagnostic tools to ensure that you are able to put these ideas into practice. Throughout this book, we will also be looking at how companies such as BP, Goldman Sachs, Nokia, and Linux have developed core organizational and operational processes to realize their competitive potential by igniting Hot Spots.

In designing for the emergence of Hot Spots, the ability to recognize and implement best practices from other companies is crucial. However, a word of warning is warranted. My research into the emergence of Hot Spots reveals that although the search for and adoption of best-practice processes is indeed necessary, it is not sufficient. On the contrary, even though importing and institutionalizing best-practice ideas and processes is important, other types of processes, which I call *signature processes,* can also be crucial. Indeed, it is your company's unique bundle of signature processes, combined with industry's best practices, that will ultimately create the context in which Hot Spots emerge.

Signature Processes

I use the term *signature* to describe the way in which these processes embody a company's character. The term signifies the idiosyncratic, unique, and essentially personal nature of these processes. These signature processes arise from passions and interests *within* the company, rather than from concepts of best practice from *outside* the company. So while one task of every executive is to find and adapt best practices—in a sense, to "bring the outside in"—an added critical task of management is to be able to learn to identify and preserve the company's own signature processes. This added duty might be thought of as the need to "bring the inside out."

The distinction between a signature process and an industry best practice is not absolute, however. In particular, if a company's signature processes prove especially advantageous, they may be imitated by other companies so often that they eventually become known as best practices.

	Best Practice	Signature Processes
Origin	Starts with external and internal search for best-practice processes	Evolves from a company-specific history
Development	"Bringing the outside in"; needs careful adaptation and alignment to the business goal and industry context	"Bringing the inside out"; needs championing by executives
Core	Shared knowledge from across the sector	Values of the executive and the company

Figure 1.5 Best Practices and Signature Processes

Toyota's lean production is an example of a process that began as a signature process for the company. It was capable of creating enormous energy and potential Hot Spots by espousing the values and aspirations of the firm's leaders. Over time, many other companies sought, not always successfully, to adopt the process of lean manufacturing.

This subtle but crucial difference between standard best-practice processes and unique signature processes (see Figure 1.5) was clear when I took a closer look at companies in which Hot Spots emerge on a frequent basis. In many of these companies, there are practices and processes that are surprising and intriguing.

Chapters 2 and 3 take a closer look at a Hot Spot in Nokia that spanned from Finland to China. When we examined the context that shapes the emergence of Hot Spots at Nokia, we discovered that the company's structural architecture plays a crucial role. Chapter 4 examines what it is about the boundary-spanning aspects of Nokia's structure that enables Hot Spots to emerge. In essence, it is its modularity, which allows frequent restructuring. This structure is unique and has a profound impact on the cooperative mindset of the company. It also affects the precision with which boundary spanning can occur. This modularity is a highly idiosyncratic practice. Best practices suggest that organizational restructuring should take place as infrequently as possible in order to maintain a relatively stable organization and minimize confusion. So why restructure frequently? At BP, as you will see in the next chapter, "peer assist" and peer-based bonuses have a critical and positive impact on cooperation and the exchange of knowledge. But again, best practices in performance management require that managers be responsible for what they can personally affect. So why reward people on the performance of their peers who are outside of their own direct line of accountability?

And yet Nokia and BP—both highly successful companies abounding with Hot Spots—adopt processes that differ significantly from general views of best practices. And perhaps even more surprisingly, the executives involved in these processes believe that they are a key part of the company's success.

The reason lies in the idiosyncrasy of these signature processes and in their potential to create the energy to drive high performance. This idiosyncrasy is a direct embodiment, a "signature," of the history and values of the company and its top executive team. The combination of values, experience, and passion enables these idiosyncratic processes to flourish against all odds.

Adopting best-practice processes gets a company to a level playing field. Yet the very nature of best practices, drawn as they are from a common pool of industry knowledge, means that the adopters of best practices are always susceptible to being copied by others that catch up with them. In contrast, the signature processes at these companies are so idiosyncratic and so much a part of the organizational heritage and values that the signature processes are difficult for competitors to replicate.

Signature processes develop from the heritage and values of the company, and it is the philosophy and wisdom of the executive team that shape them. At BP, the "peer-assist" signature process originated not in industry best practices but in the values and beliefs of CEO John Browne and his team. Browne explains the three core premises of his philosophy: "that people worked better in smaller units, . . . that any organization of scale should create proprietary knowledge through learning, . . . [and] that there is a very different interaction between people of equal standing."

Signature processes are acceptable within the companies in which they develop because very often they have grown as the company grows and are associated with the executive team's passion and values. They are part of the fabric, the ways of behaving, the "way we do things around here." So while the task of every executive is to find and adapt best-practice processes from outside the organization to build the strength of the company, an added critical task of management is to be able to articulate the company's signature processes.

This is a difficult task. Executives need skills in developing and encouraging *both* best practices *and* signature processes. However, much of what executives have been schooled to do in developing conventional best practices flies in the face of the creation of signature processes. In fact, our recommendations for creating signature processes reverse some of the very prescriptions of best practice. To nurture signature process development, executives should rediscover their heritage and unlock the treasures that have been languishing half-forgotten within the organization, rather than search externally as they do for best-practice processes. Managers should become sensitive to and elaborate on those processes in the company about which people are passionate and become more in tune with the organization's values and beliefs. The challenge in designing for the emergence of Hot Spots is to bring in best practices *and* discover and shape signature processes that reflect the culture of the company. We return to this challenge in Chapter 7 when we consider the five phases of designing for the emergence of Hot Spots.

The four elements of a Hot Spot together create a context in which latent energy is created and then productively released. Now that you know about the theory of Hot Spots, let's examine some actual Hot Spots. In Chapter 2, you will watch people from around the world engaging in these exciting adventures.

CHAPTER SUMMARY

GENERATING EXTRAORDINARY ENERGY

Key Points

The vitality of Hot Spots is a reflection of the latent energy that has been released within the Hot Spot. This latent energy is released as the result of a dynamic combination of three elements:

- A *cooperative mindset,* which involves intellectual capital, emotional capital, and social capital

- *Boundary spanning,* which is the depth and extent of the relationships within a Hot Spot

- *Igniting purpose,* which releases the energy within a Hot Spot through igniting questions, visions or tasks.

The capacity of the Hot Spot to create lasting value is dependent on a fourth element:

- *Productive capacity,* which is the extent to which members of the Hot Spot are skilled and competent in the five productive practices (appreciating others' talents, making commitments, resolving conflicts, synchronizing time, and establishing a rhythm).

Hot Spots are emergent phenomena that cannot be controlled or directed. Executives influence the emergence of Hot Spots by shaping context through the design of structures, practices, and processes; task design; their own skills and behavior; and the development of individuals' capabilities, particularly in boundary spanning.

THE RULES OF HOT SPOTS

Signature Processes

There is much that can be achieved to develop a context in which Hot Spots will emerge. However, although the importation of best practices is important, it is not sufficient. The new rule is to move beyond best practices to signature processes.

HOT SPOTS BURNING BRIGHT ACROSS THE WORLD

> Hot Spots = (Cooperative Mindset x Boundary Spanning x
> Igniting Purpose) x Productive Capacity[1]

EVERY MOMENT OF EVERY DAY, in every country of the world, Hot Spots are springing up. Extraordinary energy is generated, stimulating innovation and value for companies and the people who work in them. Fueled by connections and high-quality relationships, these Hot Spots are capable of generating enormous value through the power of new combinations.

Hot Spots are crucial, and the need for them has never been greater. In today's interconnected, dynamic, global, and technically enabled world, the creation of value and innovation rarely spring from isolated individual endeavors.[1]

You can find Hot Spots all over the world—just watching the world over a twenty-four-hour period provides many ideas and insights about this phenomenon. Taking a look at these Hot Spots, we can begin to answer some of the questions we might have about what they are and how we might harness their power.

⊙ Hot Questions

- Is the extent to which Hot Spots arise a function of the skills and attitudes of the people involved? Are we all cooperative and able to operate across boundaries, or are some of us more capable of working cooperatively than others?

- Do Hot Spots arise as a result of the context of the companies? We might ask, for example, what impact does the behavior of the leadership team have on the motivation to work cooperatively across boundaries?

- What of organizational structures, practices, and processes? We know, for example, that highly competitive remuneration practices that pit people against each other encourage competition. But what encourages the cooperative mindset of a Hot Spot to emerge? What are the practices beyond remuneration? If remuneration is not the key practice, what is?

- When Hot Spots stretch across boundaries—particularly country boundaries—what role does technology play in supporting these boundaryless relationships and encouraging them to develop as conduits of knowledge and learning?

- Why do Hot Spots fade?

⊙ Sunrise in Venezuela: Hot Spots Across BP

As the sun rises in the South American country of Venezuela, the day has started bright and fresh. In the offices of the multinational oil company BP, senior executive Carlos picks up a conference call from BP's office in Poland. On the other end of the line are Polly and members of her team. Polly is the business unit head of BP's Polish headquarters. Although Carlos has met Polly only a couple of times, he can hear worry and concern in her voice. A relative newcomer to the company, Polly is responsible for turning around BP's business in Poland. As she describes the situation to Carlos, it is clear that the first year of her role had been a disaster. The unit has just lost $20 million.

The problem in Poland

Poland was an important part of BP's strategy for eastern Europe. However, Polly and her team had failed to turn in the anticipated profit and in fact had racked up significant losses.[2] At this stage, Polly was unclear about what she and the team could do. The marketing plan for the country was simply not working, and the construction of the network of gas stations was running behind schedule. Polly took the initiative to contact Carlos because she had heard of his success in BP's business in Venezuela. He had built an infrastructure in record time, and the BP brand was becoming increasingly well known in the country. Polly's question to Carlos was this: Would Carlos and his team share their knowledge and insights about how to roll out the BP brand and cooperate with Polly and her team to help them turn around the business in Poland?

This is an interesting question and one to which Carlos has three possible responses. Perhaps the most obvious response is no, couched, of course, in the language of too many conflicting priorities. The second answer could be yes, but the yes of mock cooperation, with all the outward trappings of support but none of the inward commitments to action. The third response is yes including the inward commitments to action. This is the yes that marks the beginning of a possible Hot Spot. This is the response that Carlos selected.

Over the next year, the respective teams of Carlos and Polly would engage in deep collaboration. They shared ideas and insights about the roll-out of the BP brand in Venezuela, and a couple of people visited the Polish operation to make concrete suggestions about how to run the marketing project. They shared their insights about building the retail network and the tools and frameworks they had developed. Over the year, they provided the deep support and purposeful conversation that was key to Polly and her team's transforming a loss into a profit. Within two years, Polly had turned around the business in Poland and reported the business' first profit of $6 million.

When Polly placed her call, she was unsure what the response from the team in Venezuela might be. But from the perspective of Polly and her team, they had made a good move by trying to ignite a Hot Spot. Carlos and his colleagues had established a track record of being innovative and creative in the way they had tackled the business. But would Carlos and his colleagues be prepared to share their know-how and insights with a group on the other side of the world? Would they be prepared and able to create excitement capable of crossing the globe? Although cooperating would be enormously useful for Polly, the odds of Carlos and Polly combining their knowledge and insight to create value at BP were admittedly slim.

Think of the many situations in a company where personal fiefdoms and rivalries act as a powerful barrier to the sharing of knowledge that is at the heart of these Hot Spots. Even when the first move has been made, as Polly did with her call, many executives don't have the habits and competencies to pull off this kind of cross-national cooperation. This had been Polly's experience in her previous company, where such cooperation would have been unthinkable. And Polly is not alone in that conclusion. Many other executives like Polly believe that the major obstacle to the sharing of ideas and know-how within companies is the internal barriers to cross-departmental and cross-business working.[3]

If we took a purely economic view of the situation, we could assume that Carlos's motivation would be to act solely in his own self-interest. From this perspective, there is little to be gained by his cooperating with Polly. In fact, he has much to lose, since he may be giving to Polly knowledge that has value to him, and there may be a time in the near future when he is in competition with Polly for the next promotion.

Yet Polly and Carlos were able to go against the odds. Where we might have predicted a lukewarm reaction, they created a Hot Spot across the globe. In fact, they are not alone at BP. Our research turned up Hot Spots all over the company.

Executive behavior

At BP, the behavior of the leadership team and organizational practices played a major role in designing for the emergence of Hot Spots. In fact, for Polly, this was particularly crucial because in her previous job, she would never have cooperated to the same extent. There was something about BP that encouraged her. But what? To understand this, we had to look beyond Polly and Carlos, beyond Poland and Venezuela, to the current and past leadership team of BP and to the signature processes of the company. CEO John Browne's deep commitment to sharing knowledge played a key role in encouraging boundary spanning and the cooperative mindset throughout BP. Browne has a fundamental point of view about organizations and how they prosper. He and his team believe that learning is crucial to business performance and that people learn more from each other in a peer-to-peer relationship than they do from their boss in a subordinate-to-boss relationship. This belief has infused a number of the practices and processes that have been developed at BP over the last couple of decades and have significantly aided the emergence of Hot Spots. Perhaps the most crucial signature process has been peer assist.

BP's signature process: peer assist

John Browne oversaw the development of BP's prototype knowledge management and organizational learning program when he headed BP Exploration (BPX) in the early 1990s. He decided to transfer the approach to the whole company when he became CEO in 1995. Rather than installing a new set of information systems, Browne's first initiative was to emphasize a practice known within BP as "peer assist." This was a small-scale project that encouraged business units to reach out to other BP operations that had the expertise to help solve particular problems. Cutting through formal layers and complex procedures, the process became an accepted way of doing business, and managers soon recognized that it was not culturally acceptable to refuse a request for help.

By the time Polly joined BP, peer assist had become an important part of the company context. The business units of BP, of which there are about 150 at any one time, are grouped into what is termed "peer groups." Each peer group typically contains about thirteen business units. These are business units at similar stages of their life cycle (start-up, new production, ongoing operations, late life cycle) and facing similar strategic and technical challenges. One such peer group contains both Polly's unit and Carlos's. Members of the peer groups, like Polly and Carlos, are encouraged and guided to actively share knowledge with each other and to support each other in any way they can. They do this by engaging in a formal review of each other's goals for the next year, a process known as "peer challenge." Every business unit is responsible for achieving its own goals as well as for achieving the peer group's collective goals. The failure of one business unit in a peer group is viewed as a failure of all the units in that group. To continuously improve the performance of the business units, the top three business units in the peer group are responsible for assisting the bottom three units in the group. Deputy CEO Rodney Chase elaborates:

> One of the things that we find when we talk to other companies is that they disbelieve us when we say that our performance units have a high capacity and bias to improve one another. The point is [the performance units] have to do that or they can't meet their goals, because

they have performance outputs for the peer group. Today the top three business units in the peer group are responsible for the improvement of the bottom three. That's how they work in a structural sense. They are measured for it.

This practice is unique to BP. It plays an enormously important role in motivating Polly and Carlos and ensures that Hot Spots ignite throughout the company. As Polly explains, "First, the team that has asked for the peer assist obtains strategic and operational insight from the most respected experts in BP. Second, it is a development opportunity for the people who participate."

For Polly, the context created at BP played a huge role in her ability and capacity to develop connectivity with Carlos and his team. The context of BP served to amplify Polly's natural tendencies to be cooperative, just as the context in her previous company had stifled them.

What we saw at BP began to give some insight into the questions I had posed about Hot Spots. Polly and Carlos demonstrated that people in companies are capable of behaving in a way that goes far beyond self-interest. It showed the impact of practices and processes on the motivation and capacity to create Hot Spots, and it began to draw our attention to what was special. It was through BP we got our first inkling of signature processes.

The role of boundary spanners in Hot Spots

The context of BP played a crucial role in the emergence of the Hot Spot between Poland and Venezuela. But it was more than that. Something about the nature and experience of Polly and Carlos made a difference. Part of the difference was their personalities, their preferences, and their attitudes toward others. Both Polly and Carlos are particularly adept at working cooperatively. This was partly personality and partly a history of being boundary spanners. Both have a great deal of experience working across boundaries, and rather than staying within a single function, they had moved across functions, companies, and countries. As they had spanned these boundaries, they had built over time a wide network of friends and acquaintances with different outlooks and ways of seeing the world. As a result of their boundary spanning, both Polly and Carlos had developed skills and competencies in working cooperatively with people very different from themselves.

They had developed the skills of masterful conversation, of making commitments and facing up to the tensions and conflicts that inevitably arise in cross boundary working. Polly, for example, is adept at discovering what others know and is always willing to introduce her acquaintances and friends to each other. We discovered in our large-scale research project that boundary spanners like Polly and Carlos seem to play a crucial role in igniting Hot Spots and ensuring that the value of the whole is greater than the sum of the parts. Without people like Polly and Carlos, the social connectivity of Hot Spots withers away. The boundary spanners are the purveyors of friendships, the introducers, and the connectors.

I leave the last word about the BP Hot Spot to Deputy CEO Rodney Chase:

> *For a global institution, we are very nimble. When we want something to happen around the world, we can get all the swallows in our worldwide organization to flip like that. They can go in this direction; they can go in that direction. How does it happen? I have no idea. It is some combination of informal word of mouth; networks, which are encouraged; informal networks based on career friendships or based on professional groupings or based on clubs on the intranet. If you've got an important message that needs to get out in the firm, it will happen in twenty-four hours. And you can be certain that every thinker in the organization will have heard about it and will be thinking about it. It means that the forces for inertia have been largely swept away.*

Noon in Beijing: Hot Spots Across Nokia

At twelve o'clock sharp, the videoconferencing facilities begin to flicker in Nokia's office in downtown Beijing.[4] On the other end of the link in Nokia's Helsinki office are Pertti and his team. Pertti is one of the technical geniuses of the Finnish mobile phone company, but today he is gloomy.

Nokia's challenge in Asia

The message from the Helsinki office is clear. Earlier that year, Nokia had rejoiced when sales figures showed that the company had captured a significant percentage of the rapidly growing Asian market. However, as time went on, that delight had begun to falter. Nokia's senior team in Asia had watched in horror as their competitors' newly launched clamshell phone had stolen market share from them. For Pertti and his Chinese colleagues, this was a real blow. Pertti felt the blow particularly hard. His passion had always been technical excellence, and he knew that the functionality and technical specifications of the Nokia phone were superior to all of its competitors.

For the next three hours, the Finnish and Chinese teams talked long and hard about the reality of the situation. For the members of the Asian marketing team in the Beijing conference room, the issue was clear. In their view, Nokia's failure in the marketplace was not a reflection of the technical qualities of the phone. They knew as well as Pertti that Nokia's product was functionally superior. As the afternoon wore on, they went on to explain to the Finnish team that the failure was one of consumer preference and choice. In a market where mobile phones had suddenly emerged as a fashion item, the Nokia design was looking increasingly dated and uncool. The team in Helsinki may have innovated around product performance but had not become close enough to their Asian consumers to innovate around product design.

Reflecting on the videoconference, Pertti reminded himself that this was not the first time that Nokia faced a challenge of this magnitude. Many of the team members gathered together in the Helsinki room that afternoon could remember when the disintegration of the company's supply chain in the 1990s had brought the company to the point of bankruptcy. So there was courage in the room. There was also deep concern and anxiety.

Innovating around the product specifications and launching a new product in record time would require all the company's innovative and creative genius and insight. That went far beyond the people in the rooms in Helsinki and Beijing. It would require boundaryless cooperation between Nokia's research teams in Finland and its joint-venture partners with design expertise.

The Finnish advantage

The likelihood is that Pertti is more likely to cooperate than many other people. Why? It is not his past experiences or even his individual personality. It is his nationality. Pertti is a Finn and comes from one of the West's most cooperative and collaborative societies.[5] Living in one of the most inhospitable places in Europe, with winter temperatures consistently below freezing, the Finns have developed a deep sense of community and support. In fact, the Finnish values of teamwork and cooperation form the bedrock of Nokia, Finland's most prestigious company and one of the most admired companies in the world.

So Pertti was predisposed to behave in a cooperative manner. When we took a closer look at Nokia, we found a whole raft of practices and processes that supported his predisposition. These helped bring greater insight into the question of habits and competencies. What we discovered was that

Pertti and many of his colleagues had developed day-to-day behaviors that enabled them to cooperate more successfully.

A portfolio of cooperative practices

Nokia's developmental practices and processes encourage cooperation and discourage aggressive competition. From the time Pertti joined Nokia, he had been taught to behave cooperatively. He watched the company's leaders working cooperatively. Even the company's remuneration practices rewarded team rather than individual performance.

Thus the combination of Pertti's Finnish predisposition, his initial socialization period at Nokia, the role models in the company, and its remuneration practices ensured that cooperation had become the norm. By now, not only was Pertti *motivated* to behave cooperatively, but he was also *skilled* at cooperation—particularly the resolution of conflicts and the making of commitments that we found to be key to skillful boundaryless cooperation.

The challenge of Hot Spots

Will the Finland-China link become a Hot Spot? Will the teams at Nokia be able to pull this off? Or will they be consigned to the second-rung position in the race for potentially the largest mobile phone market in the world? As at BP, the challenge is fundamentally a challenge of a mindset of cooperation, cross-boundary working, and an igniting purpose. Are the many partners involved in making the new design a reality willing to engage in deep cooperation? Do they have the competencies, skills, and habits to actively cooperate on aspects of this complex task? Does Nokia possess the techniques and capabilities to coordinate the activities of multiple teams on opposite sides of the world? As at BP, our research revealed that the odds were stacked against success. Even in a culture of respect and teamwork, much can go wrong.

These groups in Helsinki and Beijing needed to be particularly skillful if they were to pull this off. Yet they did just that. Over the next three months, the teams in Finland and Asia developed a Hot Spot of extraordinary activity, excitement, and innovation. Building on Nokia's unique modular structure and its commitment to trust and relationships, the teams were able to achieve the boundaryless cooperation that became crucial to the success of the company in the hypercompetitive Asian market.

Within a year, Nokia had recovered from its stumble. Pertti and his team revamped the phone designs and ended up grabbing 35 percent of the market in Asia.

◉ Early Evening in London: Hot Spots at OgilvyOne

Later that evening, the sun has set on the rainy streets of London. Nigel—chairman of the London office of OgilvyOne, part of the giant advertising agency WPP—walks across a crowded room in central London. He chats briefly with colleagues before shaking the hand of Tim and exchanging a few brief words. Today is a big day for Nigel. It has marked the culmination of four months of hard work. Over the past four months, Nigel has been actively planning a merger with NoHo Digital, an interactive marketing company. Both Nigel and Tim, the CEO of NoHo Digital, are convinced of the benefit of the merger. In a world becoming ever more digital, this was potentially a match made in heaven. The merger would bring together the advertising might of WPP with the technical savvy of NoHo Digital. As advertising revenues come less and less from old-style print and television advertisements, the merger would position OgilvyOne in the booming digital market. Over the months, Nigel and Tim had talked at length about their plans to combine their skill sets and mindsets to create value through targeted and customized advertising.

The merger

Igniting a Hot Spot that spanned the two companies was never going to be easy. As in the cases of BP and Nokia, the odds are against them. They could well follow the path of many other mergers, where the aspirations for value creation significantly exceeded the reality of delivery. Nigel knows as well as anyone that to succeed, he will have to go against the grain. Fully 80 percent of the anticipated benefits of mergers and joint ventures fail to materialize. Nigel and Tim both understand how hard their task will be. Even that morning, one of Tim's most talented software wizards had angrily declared that the takeover was simply David and Goliath—the mighty WPP overwhelming the tiny NoHo Digital. He had vowed never to cooperate with WPP, and Tim was aware that many others felt the same way.[6]

For Tim, creating a Hot Spot with Nigel and the teams at OgilvyOne was never going to be a straightforward matter. He knows that there are important factions in the company who are not entirely comfortable with the acquisition. Last week, Rajit, one of the young members of the NoHo Digital team, had come to see him and spelled out their concerns. Beyond their general discomfort at merging with what they saw as a dinosaur, they also worried that their unique skills would be diluted. As Rajit poignantly put it, "You know, if we work closely with the other company and show them what we are doing, that puts us, particularly the younger team, at a disadvantage. We don't know if in the next cutback they won't fire us. We are in danger of losing our unique skills, and why would we want to do this?" Tim had acknowledged Rajit's point of view. By sharing their unique knowledge with the OgilvyOne teams, they did indeed run the risk of diluting their own value, of losing all the things they held dear. Tim is acutely aware that even if he personally wants to work cooperatively with Nigel, and he believes he does, the challenge will be to bring along a group of people, some of whom are deeply suspicious of the motives of OgilvyOne. Beyond the issues of motivation, he is also worried about the sheer logistics of pulling the two groups together. Luckily, the major offices for both companies are in London, but the NoHo employees cherish their office and would be reluctant to leave. Yet over the next few months, these two men would work with their respective teams to establish a Hot Spot between their two companies that became the envy of the advertising world.

The role of technology in Hot Spots

Since the early 1990s, enormous efforts at OgilvyOne had gone into the technology and attributes that encourage the boundaryless nature of Hot Spots. The 1990s saw a massive investment in technology that enabled teams at OgilvyOne to connect with themselves and their clients. This had required building an integrated system called Truffles. Beyond a database and an expert system overlay for testing ideas and hypotheses, Truffles provides opportunities for jointly creating new ideas through a variety of chat rooms, bulletin boards, and dedicated forums.

The Truffles name comes from a statement of OgilvyOne's founder, David Ogilvy: "I prefer the discipline of knowledge to the anarchy of ignorance, and we pursue knowledge the way a pig pursues truffles." Supported by sixty knowledge officers across the company, the Truffles initiative is the product of years of documenting the accumulated intellectual capital of the company. It is also a living forum for creating and sharing new ideas and the platform from which Hot Spots can develop.

Crossing boundaries

At OgilvyOne, the experience of being in a Hot Spot is fundamentally an experience of being connected—to have flexible networks with people, both in the Hot Spot and beyond. It is this social connectivity that enables people within a Hot Spot to link, embed, and leverage their diverse knowledge and expertise.

The intellectual capital and links to it via Truffles ensure that ideas and knowledge are shared across the Hot Spot. But the success of a Hot Spot requires more than this. Fundamentally, it is the "soft bonds" between people that support the spirit of sharing and using knowledge that are crucial to the experience of being in a Hot Spot.

Even at the beginning of the merger talks, Nigel and his colleagues had realized that although the technological platform would be an important prerequisite in support of the Hot Spot, it would not be sufficient. What would also be crucial to the company efforts to create value was its capacity to support the creation of cooperative relationships. To do this, Nigel and his colleagues had created many conversation forums—Friday morning breakfast meetings, top-level "board away" days, and more. Using the motto "The most important role of the manager is to create friendships," the senior leaders invested considerable personal time developing the internal trust that allows Hot Spots to emerge.

This was the technology and cultural background that Nigel took with him when he first met Tim. What it meant was that over the coming months, Nigel spent a considerable amount of time building a relationship with Tim. The discussions were as much personal as they were strategic. The result of the friendship they built was manifest immediately after the acquisition was finalized. Within two weeks, NoHo Digital's employees were not only using Truffles but were also contributing new information and techniques to the database for use by all OgilvyOne employees. Once the acquisition of NoHo Digital had taken place, the integration of skills and competencies was rapid and successful, and later that year, the advertising magazine *Adweek* described the company merger as "one of the premier models of how a traditional ad agency can operate successfully in the nontraditional world of cyberspace."[7]

Early Morning in Singapore: Hot Spots at Linux

Around two in the morning, Amit finally switches off the computer in his small room in Singapore. This has been a long night. Since seven that evening, he has been wrestling with a problem a colleague in San Francisco had sent earlier in the day. By day, Amit is a software engineer for one of the large consulting companies, posted from Mumbai to Singapore for a couple of years. By night, he is a Linux warrior. Like thousands of people around the world, Amit dedicates a significant amount of his own time to keeping the Linux system operating.[8] He shares much in common with these thousands of people; the vast majority of Linux programmers are men in their mid-twenties, and like more than half of his colleagues at Linux, Amit works in IT.

The Linux army

Together, this vast army of people has created one of the wonders of the corporate world—a community that rivals Microsoft, built by volunteers. Linux is an operating system that was initially created as a hobby by Linus Torvalds, a student at the University of Helsinki in Finland. He had begun work in 1991 and in 1994 released the Linux kernel. The kernel, at the heart of all Linux systems, is developed and released under a general public license, and its source code is freely available to everyone. It is this kernel that forms the base around which a Linux operating system is developed. There are now hundreds of companies, organizations, and individuals that have released their own version of the operating system.

This open-source system is freely available, and its functionality, adaptability, and robustness make it the main alternative to proprietary Unix and Microsoft operating systems. More than a decade after its initial release, Linux is now a platform adopted worldwide for use in home and office desktop operating systems and is embedded in many appliances and devices. It is also increasingly used by corporations. Investment banks such as Merrill Lynch, Goldman Sachs, and Crédit Suisse First Boston are all running their billion-dollar financial transactions on a Linux platform.

Like the other thousands of people working on Linux, Amit is a volunteer. He gives five to ten hours a week, free of charge, to maintain the system. The idea of volunteering for work was not at the top of his agenda until he spent a year in Atlanta. It was during his IT studies in the early 1990s that he got to hear about Linus Torvalds and Richard Stallman's attack on closed proprietary programs such as Microsoft and Sun Microsystems. Stallman, the seminal figure in the open-source culture, had imagined groups or individuals building on each other's development. Eventually his code had been paired with code written by Linus Torvalds to become the Linux operating system. Back then, the system was regarded as a geeky. But by 2004, it had emerged as a credible option to proprietary operating systems. With open-source systems, users are allowed to freely copy the program, modify it, and release these changes back into the programming community since contribution and collaboration are two tenets at the foundation of the movement.

Linux is not a plaything of the technical wizards of the world. Amit is justly proud of the fact that many governments around the world have chosen Linux's open-source software, despite Microsoft's muscle. In fact, the Singapore government was offering tax incentives to companies who used Linux instead of alternative proprietary solutions. Initially, the decision of companies and governments to use Linux had been based on cost savings, but now more and more businesses have come to regard it as more flexible.

Igniting Hot Spots

What ignites a Hot Spot? This is a crucial question. It is clear that Hot Spots cannot be commanded to appear. Yet it is also clear that the context, such as the values of Nokia or the practices of BP, can play a key role. But this context is not enough; Hot Spots need to be ignited.

Hot Spots can be ignited by what may seem like an insolvable problem that only a collection of engaged and excited people can solve. This intellectual curiosity and the unsolved problem seem key to the Linux Hot Spot. At the start of the Linux history, ignition was the result of a combination of a seemingly unsolvable technical problem (the creation of open-source software) and an intriguing thought (shared by volunteers strung out around the world). For Amit, the joy of a Hot Spot comes on a daily basis from solving the many problems that occur in the software. Some problems seem at first unsolvable, but the combination of intellectual insight and skills in the community often lead to solutions.

Amit takes enormous pride that he and his colleagues use their insights and intellect to ensure that the Linux system's stability remains superior to that of Microsoft. For Amit, this is one of the most intellectually exciting aspects of his life. The peer review that he and his colleagues engage in makes the open-source software less prone to bugs. That peer review process is built on the knowledge and talents of the whole community. A very precise intellectual framing combined with an extensive network of knowledge ignites the Hot Spots in the Linux community. The vast majority of the members of the Linux community are IT engineers. As a consequence, they have the same skills, speak the same language, and follow the same disciplines. There is a great deal of shared know-how and mutual understanding, respect, and ways of working.

One of the bonds that hold Amit to the Linux community is the opportunity he has to learn from others. So even though not everyone in a Hot Spot needs to be operating at the same high level of intellectual curiosity, some certainly do. Ultimately, their intellectual curiosity is driven by their own needs and desires to become active and lifelong learners. We found that the context of the organization could amplify this tendency through training and educational opportunities and through stretching and meaningful roles. Beyond this, the intellectual sparkle of a Hot Spot comes from engaged and excited, inquisitive and curious people.

Amit enjoys his reputation as a competent contributor and goes to great lengths to ensure that every piece of code he writes is as perfect as it can be. He knows that with every line he writes, his reputation is at stake. When people make a contribution, their input and ideas are readily and routinely acknowledged. The Linux community uses a particular format to acknowledge the contributions of its members. So as Amit works on solving a particular problem, his contribution is acknowledged through the placing of his e-mail identifier at the end of the communication.

What Amit and Linux helped me understand is that often the ignition of a Hot Spot comes from a belief, a passion, a point of view, a question that is often challenging and audacious. The Linux Hot Spots are ignited by fundamental questions about the nature of software and who owns it. They are ignited by a belief in open-source software and the free availability of this wonderful resource. They are also ignited by the sheer complexity and ingenuity of thousands of people working collaboratively.

When relationships are virtual

One of the fascinating aspects of the Linux community is that most of its members have never met. Amit has met few of his Linux colleagues, so one might expect that his experience of being in a Hot Spot had limited connectivity, but that is not the case. For Amit, the Linux community is constantly ignited by the social connectivity of relationships. Unlike the face-to-face interactions of Nigel and Tim at OgilvyOne or the executive conference and videoconferencing of Polly and Carlos at BP, the relationships and connectivity that Amit has with other members of the Linux community are essentially mediated by e-mail. It helps, of course, that the vast majority of the Linux community consists of technically savvy GenXers—and IT experts to boot. This has meant that for Amit and his colleagues, the experience of being in a Hot Spot remains an experience of connectivity. For them, this social connectivity is mediated by the intranet. In fact, they are able to create connectivity with perhaps as much finesse as baby boomers Nigel and Tim do in a crowded room in the center of London. What holds this virtual social connectivity together is the experience of being in a place that has intellectual sparkle. Here is a vast army of young people working in small Hot Spots to solve very complex, exciting problems and feeling a great deal of pride in their capacity to do so.

For now, the challenge Amit faces is solving the problem at hand. Earlier in the day, an attacker had penetrated one of the Linux servers. The breach had been traced to a vulnerable part of the Linux kernel. He had received an e-mail from one of the well-known programmers in California about the location of the breach. Amit is one of more than two thousand people around the world who operate as patch contributors. Tonight he is working on writing a patch that can go out in the early morning to the user-developers to test. Amit knows that it will take no more than a day for the patch to be posted to the Web site and distributed to Linux users worldwide.[9]

The Decay of Hot Spots: DEC, 1980–1990

For Amit, the intellectual challenge and opportunity to grow are central to his experience of being in a Hot Spot. Yet intellectual sparkle alone is not enough to keep a Hot Spot energized. If it were just about intellectual sparkle, then Digital Equipment Corporation (DEC) and all the Hot Spots it contained at one point in its history would not have disappeared as an independent company.[10]

Even in the late 1980s, when DEC's competitive problems had already become manifest, it still had the very best people in the business and the intellectual curiosity that fueled Hot Spots. Given its deep roots in MIT and its historical reputation for technological excellence, it had been the most preferred employer of the best computer science graduates for over two decades.

It was some of those people and their intellect and insight that after leaving DEC, created the Hot Spot that resulted in the Windows NT project at Microsoft, that built the Hot Spots that helped Compaq achieve leadership in the PC market, and the Hot Spots that eventually revitalized IBM's position in the network business. Yet the Hot Spots in DEC decayed, and eventually the company decayed with them. This was in spite of the formidable intellectual capacity it commanded until its last days and in spite of the Hot Spots that marked the early years.

Relationships begin to atrophy

People at DEC possessed the intellectual sparkle that excited them to engage, but the company ultimately died because of the steady erosion of the connectivity within the Hot Spot. What happened? Clearly, connectivity was a crucial element of the experience of being at DEC in the 1980s. In fact, it was this social connectivity that served as the glue that held many highly talented people together. Over time, like the Linux community, DEC had become a vast network of relationships both within the company and with its customers, OEMs, and suppliers. Despite a complex matrix structure built around geography, products, and functions, the organization had remained fluid and flexible. Why was this so? It was in part a tribute to the many team leaders and members of DEC who managed to create trust and goodwill. It was also a result of the dense web of informal relationships that had been built up over three decades of stable employment and frequent internal movements. In the 1980s, the Hot Spots in DEC had reached through to its customers, OEMs. and suppliers.

By the mid-1980s, however the experience of social connectivity that had bonded members of the Hot Spots together had begun to fail. The internal relationships had begun to atrophy amid growing formalization and an expanding corporate bureaucracy. A 1990 reorganization around three different kinds of business units finally destroyed the historical stock of social connectivity that had been such an important part of the experience of DEC and such a crucial part of the boundaryless cooperation of the Hot Spots. From a dense network of reciprocal relationships, the company became highly fragmented. Worse still, a complex system of cross-business trading of resources and products created a culture of transactions and competition where a culture of trust and reciprocity had once flourished. The experiences of trust and reciprocity had been overwhelmed by a system of transactions. These simply served to pit members against each other. What had been a Hot Spot experience had cooled into a Big Freeze of corporate bureaucracy.

Practices and processes can serve to amplify the natural cooperative nature of people. At BP, we saw how practices such as peer assist created a forum in which sharing knowledge became natural and trust became amplified. Practices and processes can also have the opposite effect. At DEC, the importation of best-practice competitive performance measures and structures from other companies simply served to damp down natural cooperation and trigger competitive behaviors that accentuated the tensions and conflicts within the company.

Purpose erodes

Ultimately, the Hot Spots at DEC died—and eventually, so did the company—because of the erosion of purpose. By the late 1980s, the spirit of David against the IBM Goliath was gone in what had become the world's second-largest computer company. DEC employees without clarity and vision began to lose their way and with it a sense of what held them together. The clarity of a vision and a shared agenda had begun to be lost. With no resolution of the conflicting possibilities, the Hot Spots began to cool down. With fundamentally different and conflicting goals, the trust-based internal networks of the Hot Spots were destroyed, leaving people demotivated and disenfranchised.

Just because a place is filled with Hot Spots at the start does not mean they will continue to burn bright. At DEC, we saw that the intellectual sparkle began to tarnish, the social connectivity began to atrophy, and the purpose dulled as the culture turned increasingly transactional.

Keeping Hot Spots Alive

Does the fate that befell DEC await the Linux community? One can speculate whether the emotional passion of Linux will erode over time, taking with it the possibility of Hot Spots naturally flaring up across the world. When Amit joined the community five years ago, it was full of excited and inspired people. Now it is one of the fastest-growing operating systems in the world. As it has become more mainstream, companies such as IBM and Red Hat have increasingly made money out of the code that was developed free by people like Amit and others in the open-source community. Will Amit continue to participate in the effort, or will he begin to demand compensation for the contribution he and others have made to the bottom line of these companies? Will these economic trends lead Amit and others to abandon their passion for Linux and their emotional attachment to open sourcing? If this were to occur, the Hot Spots at Linux may not fade, but they are likely to evolve into more conventional situations involving task forces and project teams within companies with objectives and compensation structures.

People develop and participate in Hot Spots because they are stimulating, exciting, connecting, and purposeful. It is the energy generated by this connectivity of human capital that ensures Hot Spots are sources of real productivity and potentially of great innovation. Looking closely at the experiences within Hot Spots gives us a better idea about what they are, why they emerge, and why they ultimately revive or atrophy. To understand how to create Hot Spots in organizations, we need to look in more detail at the elements and consider the organizational practices and processes that are associated with them. To do this, we return to the four elements.

CHAPTER SUMMARY

HOT SPOTS BURNING BRIGHT ACROSS THE WORLD

Key Points

- Anyone can flourish in a Hot Spot. However, the capacity and desire to work cooperatively across boundaries—to be a boundary spanner—can make a significant positive impact.

- The context of the organization plays a key role in terms of practices, processes, values, and leadership behavior and assumptions.

- It is the dynamic combination of a cooperative mindset, cross-boundary working, and an igniting purpose that can result in the emergence of a Hot Spot.

- Hot Spots fade when any of these elements decays.

3

THE FIRST ELEMENT: A COOPERATIVE MINDSET

Hot Spots = (<u>Cooperative Mindset</u> x Boundary Spanning x Igniting Purpose) x Productive Capacity

THE CAPACITY TO WORK cooperatively is at the core of Hot Spots. In a real sense, the value from Hot Spots arises in the *space between people*. Fundamentally, Hot Spots are places of cooperative relationships; some of these relationships will be transitory, and others will be strong and last over time. The friendships that form in the context of a Hot Spot increase the value of a Hot Spot and are a source of real joy to the people involved.

These relationships emerge at least in part as a result of a *cooperative mindset*—a basic assumption and expectation of ourselves and others that we will behave in a supportive and cooperative manner. Perhaps one of the most profound insights from our research is that this cooperative mindset comes to the fore in a unique way in every situation and every company. It would be both naive and foolish to suppose that a couple of simple interventions could change what is fundamentally a cultural aspect of people, groups, and companies. When a mindset of cooperation emerges, it does so as the result of an ongoing interplay between assumptions, practices, norms, language, and behavior. To illustrate this subtle interplay, let us begin this exploration of the willingness to cooperate with a look into the origins of its opposite, a corrosive and competitive mindset.

Again and again in our research on Hot Spots, we discovered that at the heart of the failure to develop a cooperative mindset are the barriers created by competitive behaviors. In many cases, these barriers are erected in an almost unwitting and unconscious manner. Very few of the executives we interviewed would actually say, "We believe that unrestrained competition is the best way to attain high performance in this company, and we encourage our people to be competitive." In fact, in a number of companies we studied, we found that executives hoped for cooperation and yearned for Hot Spots. Yet in their day-to-day behavior, their underlying assumptions and attitudes told a different story.

Take, for example, Peter, a senior executive in a large company that manufactures and services high-technology equipment. The company's workforce is made up of a small research and development function, a marketing function, a logistics function, and a large sales function. When we spoke with Peter, his words were all about cooperation. In fact, he directed our attention to one of the points in the company's value statement: "Teamwork is crucial to the performance of this company." We were not surprised, then, that Peter's assumption—and ours—was that the company would abound with cooperative Hot Spots.

Our analysis of the culture and norms of the company showed that this was not the case. In fact, what we saw instead was the Big Freeze. In our interviews with the engineers, many commented that the senior team, including Peter, were aggressive toward each other. The stories we heard were not Hot Spot stories; instead they were tales of senior team showdowns in the corridor. There was even a widely held perception that a number of senior team members refused to speak to each other—such was the extent of the turf battles between them. So despite the official rhetoric of cooperation and collaboration, the corporate culture had created something quite the opposite.

Corporate rhetoric versus individual reality

The rhetoric and written values of this company extolled teamwork and cooperation; at the same time, however, the deeper "unwritten rules" told a different story. The unwritten rules are the underlying assumptions that actually drive the company. These are the rules that new hires learn within their first month in the company. They are the way of behaving, what you have to do to get along around here and get your work done. Unlike the corporate values, these unwritten rules are never formally stated, but they are clearly understood.[1]

In this company, despite the corporate rhetoric of cooperation and teamwork, the unwritten rules encouraged people to outshine everyone around them. So rather than sharing ideas and know-how, people hoarded knowledge and worked with others as little as possible. In fact, within weeks of joining the company, we found that new hires had learned to talk about cooperation but to act competitively. In this company, like other companies we studied, there was an enormous gap between the rhetoric of cooperation and the reality of competition. People had learned to hoard important knowledge. New hires began to identify with their own work group, and to be suspicious of others. Over time, they learned the habits of competition, and any cooperative habits they may have brought to the job quickly atrophied.

We saw the same phenomenon in a number of companies that had fewer than their fair share of Hot Spots. A hot question began to form: Why do companies hope for cooperation and Hot Spots while imposing competition and the Big Freeze? To find an answer, let's return to Peter's tale and figure out why Hot Spots had failed to emerge in his company.

◎ A Self-Fulfilling Prophecy: The Emergence of a Competitive Mindset

For psychologists Farizio Ferraro, Jeffrey Pfeffer, and Robert Sutton, the answer to the hot question is simple: What is occurring here is a self-fulfilling prophecy.[2] The cycle begins with the often unconscious attitudes and assumptions of executives that drive behaviors in the corporate world they create. To understand this concept better, let's see how it plays out in relation to Peter's company. To do so, we focus on the engineering team in one of the core businesses. This is a team of sixty-five engineers distributed across three states in the United States whose job is to service machines in client companies. This was one of the places Peter had hoped to find Hot Spots. Instead he found the Big Freeze.

It starts with assumptions

We began the analysis of the Big Freeze by spending time with Peter and his colleagues to try to understand how they acted and what their assumptions were. What we discovered was that the *assumptions* of the executive team were that the performance of the engineers could be motivated by the opportunity for reward. In other words, they assumed that the engineers act to maximize their own self-interest. This should not surprise us. The assumption that we are motivated by our pursuit of self-interest is the persistent model in economic theories and the operative theory for most managers. The idea here is that individuals will compete with each other to further their self-interest, often in opposition to the interests of others. In making this assumption, Peter and his colleagues would simply be following the advice of James Lincoln, of the famous Lincoln Electric Company, when he said, "Competition will mean the disappearance of the lazy and of the incompetent. . . . Competition promotes progress."[3]

Assumptions influence practices and processes

When Peter and his executive team shaped the design of the organizational practices and processes, they did so on the assumption that the engineers are motivated to maximize their self-interest. The natural implication of this assumption is to focus on performance management and to motivate the engineers by rewarding their individual efforts.

The primary object of the complex reward system designed by the HR team was to build performance by creating competition between the engineers. This was achieved by ranking the performance of individuals and then allocating the maximum bonuses to the highest-performing engineers. The measure of performance here is the number of machines serviced. Engineers who serviced the machines the fastest received the highest performance rating and the largest bonuses. By focusing on individual performance and bonus payments, Peter and his executive team were simply following the advice of James Lincoln—that the best way of creating performance is to pit people against each other.

To arrive at a calculation of the bonus, the performance management system was designed to measure the speed with which individual engineers completed their tasks and moved on to the next. The number of service calls completed per day were then tabulated, and the engineers' rankings were prominently posted each week on the wall of the employees' lounge. When opportunities for promotion came along, the engineers at the top of the ranking were regarded as the most likely candidates for management positions.

The context shapes the social norms

We might ask what impact these performance monitoring, ranking, and bonus systems have on the behavior of the service engineers. Part of the answer to this can be found in the behavior of service engineers who have been with the company for less than six months. They become rapidly aware of which aspects of their performance are rewarded and measured and who gets promoted. They learn to get their name near the top of the weekly rankings displayed on the employees' lounge wall. Most important, they learn that the best way to ensure that their name rises to the top of the ranking and to earn a big bonus is to work on their own.

As a consequence, many of the new hires struggle in the first few months. We learned that they rarely met with other engineers, and when they did, they found their colleagues pleasant but ultimately unhelpful. When they did have a problem and talked to others about it, they were directed to the service manual. As a consequence, a significant number of these new hires left within the first three months of their contract. Could it be that they left because this competitive environment did not suit them? Those who stayed enjoyed seeing their names move up the rankings and working independently.

Many of those who stayed became adept service engineers. On the occasions when the service manual did not explain what to do, they referred the problem to the head office. However, this was frowned on, so the engineers learned to make these referrals as infrequently as possible. Since performance was being measured by speed of service, engineers learned that when a machine cannot be rapidly repaired, the best strategy is to leave it. Some may have even have delved into the gentle and unobtrusive art of sabotage, putting blame on customer inexperience and moving on to the next service job. Within a relatively short period of time, these new hires—or at least the ones who stay—are doing exactly what the executives thought they would do.[4] They are operating on the basis of maximizing their own self-interest rather than cooperating and sharing knowledge with others. Thanks to this self-interested behavior, any possibility of a Hot Spot emerging begins to fade.

Social norms influence language and stories

Like their fellow engineers, the newcomers have learned a whole new language.[5] When they meet in the cafeteria or the lounge, they talk about "screwing the competition" (by which they mean the engineers on the other team) and "topping the ranking" (getting to the top of the rankings). They have also developed a whole set of language and stories about the engineers who always seem to be at the top of the rankings and the heroic actions they have taken to get there. We listened to these stories carefully because stories provide crucial insight into the norms of a company. It is through these internal myths and stories that the assumptions about work are brought into the reality of day-to-day experiences.

To understand the power of these subtle messages, let us divert for a moment into the world of what psychologists call priming. Consider for a moment an experiment a group of Stanford research psychologists set up with American college students.[6]

In the experimental situation, students are instructed to participate in a game. To one group of college students, the game is introduced as the Wall Street Game, and to the other group, it is introduced as the Community Game—same game, different name. You might anticipate that since it is the same game, both groups of students will play it the same way. But surprisingly, the Stanford psychologists found that by simply calling the game by different names, the students behaved differently. The moves they chose were different, and the way they anticipated others' moves was different.

When the game was called the Community Game, the teams promptly adopted a rule of mutual cooperation. But when the game was called the Wall Street Game, the teams rapidly became highly competitive and described the other team in oppositional terms. Simply by changing the label, the psychologists had primed the students to behave differently. When the priming is about competition, the effect is to modify and damp down cooperative behaviors and to accentuate and amplify competitive behaviors.

Practices, norms, and language influence legitimized and delegitimized behavior

By experiencing practices such as the reward and promotion system and through the more subtle primers such as language and stories, these engineers have learned what behavior is legitimized. The impact of these organizational practices and language is not to completely change their behavior; however, the effect is to manipulate their behavior by indicating what is acceptable and what is not.

Taken together, the practices and processes, symbols and language serve to accentuate what is legitimate and to make clear what is not. Delegitimized behavior is branded as inappropriate and is not reinforced. In the case of the engineers, they have learned a number of legitimized behaviors, including that it is good to hoard their insights and knowledge about how a particular problem can be fixed. They have learned that it is acceptable to openly compete with their colleagues. They have learned that it is acceptable to spend free time with their manager and that their manager will not object to disparaging comments about their colleagues. In fact, their

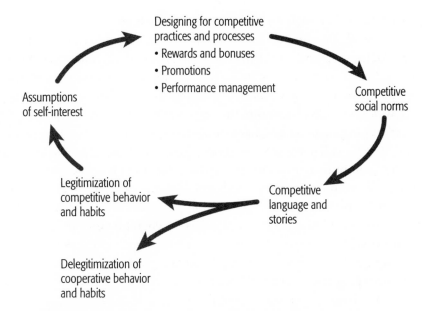

Figure 3.1 Corporate assumptions and the self-fulfilling prophecy

manager seems to find these useful. As they say, "It helps me get a feel about what is going on at the grassroots level." Over time, through watching others, they have learned what is appropriate behavior for an engineer.

They have also learned what is delegitimized, what they absolutely should not be doing. They have learned within their first weeks in the company that it is a sign of weakness to talk about the problems they face. They have learned that they would be interfering to show others how to solve their problems, that it is best to cover up problems and not even mention them to managers.

There are always unintended consequences

Figure 3.1 shows how the self-fulfilling cycle develops. Starting at the top, executives' assumptions about self-interest shape practices and processes that in turn serve to create norms of competition. These norms are communicated to new hires who over time become increasingly competitive and act in their own self-interest, simply serving to reinforce what the executive team thought all along.

The impact of this self-fulfilling prophecy is that the resilience of the company deteriorates. In part, this is a direct consequence of the hoarding of knowledge. The engineers fail to report the small problems they encounter; as a result, executives fail to spot underlying systemic technical problems. All the executive team can hope is that the research and development (R&D) function they have designed is sufficiently knowledgeable to develop new products. The task for the R&D team members will be hard, since they receive very little feedback from the engineers and hence gain scant insight into the changing needs of customers.

There are still other consequences of the self-fulfilling prophecy based on the assumption of self-interest. Where collaboration is important to the success of the endeavor, executives have to design practices and process that motivate employees to cooperate.[7] Simply put, they have to pay for cooperation. So, for example, if Peter now wants the engineers on a team to work cooperatively with each other, he will have to specify in the performance contract when and where cooperation can take place and then measure if it is occurring. In essence, he will have to put in place incentives for cooperation, since the current practices and processes have delegitimized cooperative behavior.

For Peter and his colleagues, competition has become "hard-wired" into the fabric of the whole company. It is part of the core practices and processes of the company; it is heard in the everyday language; it permeates the company premises. It becomes the air that is breathed. It is no surprise, then, that simply rewriting the value statement to include words such as *cooperation, respect,* and *trust* serves no real purpose. What is more, it seems cynical as employees observe and experience on a day-to-day basis the growing schism between the rhetoric of cooperation and the reality of competition.

The Unacceptably High Cost of a Transactional Mindset

A starting assumption of self-interest has inadvertently reduced Peter's chances of creating a cooperative and innovative company. To take the idea of self-interest and competition to its nature conclusion, let us return for a moment to the merger between OgilvyOne and NoHo Digital. You may recall that Nigel, who heads up OgilvyOne in London, is working with Tim, the founder of NoHo Digital. As the merger plays out, imagine for a moment that self-interest is the key motivator for both men as they approach the merging of their companies.

Working on the basis of self-interest, we might anticipate that Tim will ultimately be motivated to maximize the merger price of NoHo Digital. At the same time, Nigel will be working in his own self-interest and be striving to minimize the merger price. Of course, both men will be entirely rational in their decision-making process. We can predict that the merger of the two companies will inevitably create conflict as the parties attempt to maximize their own self-interest.

This creates a challenge. Simply put, how can individuals or the institutions of which they are members create the means by which performance can be maximized while minimizing the potential disadvantages of conflict? This question has taxed economists for decades. It is often posed as "How might a society of self-interested individuals be organized so that they can coexist together in mutually profitable ways?" and "What is the optimal solution to the inherent conflict between people?"

The answer to this quandary has been honed over decades. In the solution, the law and lawyers play a key role. Their job is to create contracts between the sides that specify the cost and distribution of the value of the outcomes. It is the specification of these contracts that is ultimately necessary to curb individuals' opportunism.[8] In the making of these contracts, the development of social relationships between people will be seen as harmful. This is because in this model, the assumption of human nature is that social relationships will be developed by people only in order to maximize their self-interest. Social relationships will be developed on the basis of nepotism and insider trading. These relationships, then, will ultimately threaten the effective operation of the market. As Adam Smith so poignantly expressed his own belief about self-interest, "People of the same trade seldom meet together, even for merriment or diversion, but the conversation ends in a conspiracy against the public, or in some contrivance to raise prices."[9] What Smith would have made of Linux and other voluntary communities is unclear.

If we examine the merger of OgilvyOne and NoHo Digital through the lens of the self-fulfilling prophecy in Figure 3.1, we can make various predictions. If maximization of self-interest is the primary assumption, then we could anticipate that very soon, Tim will meet with his lawyers and Nigel will meet with his lawyers as each seeks to create a form of contract that will maximize his own interests. From here, the merger will proceed by means of tough negotiations between the two teams of lawyers. In the law offices, each side will be attempting to assess the resources of the other and judge what it will gain from the exchange. Hence they are likely to be talking about quantifiable aspects such as the exchange of technology or the merging of client lists.

In other words, we can predict that the Big Freeze has begun. The spontaneity and trust of a Hot Spot, rich with relationships and intellectual stimulation, has been replaced by the transactions of lawyers.

Toyota versus General Motors

One of the most interesting features of Hot Spots is that they drive down cost by significantly reducing transaction costs. Outside a Hot Spot, transaction costs accelerate as each party tries to reduce its vulnerability in the face of uncertainty. To do this, each side spends money on negotiations, supervision, and restitution to reduce these vulnerabilities.

In a fascinating study of the U.S. economy in 2000, the Boston Consultancy Groups' Philip Evans and Bob Wolf estimated the transaction costs of U.S. businesses. They calculated that cash transaction costs alone accounted for over half the nongovernmental U.S. gross domestic product (GDP). In this situation, people spend more time negotiating and enforcing transactions than they do fulfilling them.[10]

Contrast these transaction costs with those in the Linux community, where agreements are enforced not by the sanctions of legal contracts or by the authority of the boss but by mutual trust. This mutual trust has the effect of lowering transaction costs dramatically. Teams of people have always been able to operate on the basis of trust and reciprocity. What is exciting about the Hot Spots in Linux—and BP and Nokia—is that they extend far beyond the boundaries of conventional teams, right through to people who have never even met each other.

Evans and Wolf found in their study of the Toyota production system that transaction costs fell because there was simply less to negotiate over.

In the Linux community, transaction costs approach zero. In the Toyota community, transaction costs, while not zero, are radically less than their competitors'. The transaction costs between Toyota and its first-tier suppliers are just one-eighth those of General Motors, a disparity that could be attributed directly to the different levels of trust.

Why do companies fail to create the hoped-for value in mergers, partnerships, and cross-functional work? Most employees of companies are not dumb people and are highly motivated to do the best for their companies. Who would not prefer to be in a Hot Spot than out in the freezing cold? Yet time and time again, we find the Big Freeze in place of Hot Spots. People

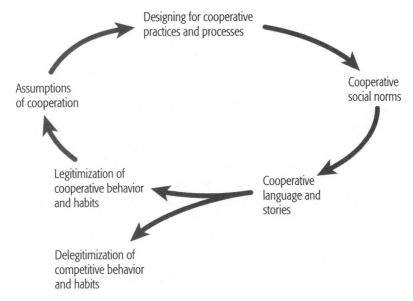

Figure 3.2 Emergence of a Cooperative Mindset: It Starts with Assumptions

behaving competitively, hoarding knowledge, not trusting each other, looking to the status quo rather than being innovative, fearful of taking risks, failing to establish the nurturing that comes from friendships, failing to engage in deep collaboration. Fundamentally, Hot Spots arise from an attitude of mind; a set of beliefs and assumptions, and a way of looking at the world. It is these beliefs and assumptions that often unconsciously determine where executives direct their resources, what they concentrate their attention on, and how they decide to act and behave toward others. The good news is that the self-fulfilling cycle can also be used in the service of Hot Spots, and we now turn to how the cooperative mindset emerges.

How a Cooperative Mindset Emerges

Now that you know how the Big Freeze and a culture of corrosive competition arises, it is time to understand how a mindset of cooperation arises. Again the answer can be found in the self-fulfilling prophecy. A cooperative mindset arises when a whole system of organizational practices, norms, language, stories, and habits are aligned.[11] The systemic nature of this is shown in Figure 3.2.

Just as assumptions drives the corrosive cycle, assumptions also drive the cooperative cycle. Of all the assumptions a leader may have, perhaps the ones most central to cooperation are assumptions about human motivation. Simply put, what motivates a person to excel? In the previous scenario, we saw that Peter and his colleagues assumed that people excel when they are competing. What other assumptions might managers make as to why people are motivated to excel?

Put another way, with regard to motivation, what stands in the place of competition? Many executives are understandably concerned that as a result of developing a mindset of cooperation, the company becomes a "country club," a place where everyone has a great time but nothing gets done. In the Hot Spots that I observed, energy was high and cooperation was productive rather than unproductive. So what has saved these companies from the country club mentality?

In these situations, the energy of the cooperative mindset comes not from a mindset of competition but rather from a mindset of excellence. The focus is on the excellence toward which people are striving together rather than the competition of beating everyone else to the goal. I am inclined here to follow Aristotle's teaching and consider the assumption that excellence has two aspects. The first is moral excellence, a striving toward a deep understanding of oneself and one's own values. The second aspect is intellectual excellence, a striving toward the maximization of one's intellectual potential. Aristotle believed that intellectual excellence is developed primarily through teaching and moral excellence through the development of habits.[12]

Assumptions about moral excellence

The assumptions executives hold regarding excellence as a driving force behind behavior cover a broad range of possibilities that include the creation of a life of meaning, the joy of friendship, and the exhilaration of success in complex and demanding tasks. Assuming that behavior is motivated by moral excellence assumes that each person who comes into the organization brings their values and assumptions with them. Executives determined to design for cooperation and for excellence will pay particular attention to who is selected to join the organization and who gets promoted. In our research, we discovered that organizations where Hot Spots flourish invest very heavily in lengthy, interactive selection processes, frequently involving both senior managers and peers with whom recruits are likely to work and often with an informal social dimension. The criteria for selection extend far beyond technical expertise, important though this is, to personal attributes such as commitment to the job and enjoyment of cooperation.

Let us digress for a moment to consider what we might be looking for in a candidate who has the potential for excellence. Aristotle identifies many qualities associated with excellence. They include courage, known to be important for sensible risk taking in innovation, and "greatness of soul," which is a sense of self-worth containing, as Aristotle put it, neither "conceitedness" nor "littleness of soul." This sense of self-respect is important to the establishment of a mindset of cooperation. It fashions the self-respect that enables each of us to recognize the contribution we personally need to make to the ongoing work of the organization. This sense of personal responsibility is particularly important in volunteer communities such as Linux.

Assumptions about intellectual excellence

One aspect of being in a Hot Spot is what I earlier termed "intellectual sparkle." It was this sparkle that motivated people to engage in the Hot Spot. They had a belief that they could learn from others and develop their own intellectual capabilities by being mentored and coached by others. The practices and processes associated with intellectual excellence include, for example, ways of reasoning and different modes of thinking and behaving. The aim is not only to develop the individual mind but also to provide the foundation for a meeting of minds.

Assumptions Influence Practices and Processes

In the competitive cycle—the self-fulfilling prophecy—we saw the crucial role that executive behavior and individual bonus payments have on the emergence of self-interested behavior. In my research on Hot Spots, I made several important discoveries:

- A cooperative mindset does not arise from a single characteristic; instead it arises as a result of a whole system of practices, processes, behaviors, and norms. Cooperation is not built; it emerges.

- Although practices and processes such as training and rewards can play a key role in supporting the cooperative mindset, ultimately cooperation is learned from others. In this learning process, the behavior of peers and the executive team plays a central role. Our research showed that of all the factors that influenced the cooperative mindset, the cooperative behavior of the senior team was one of the most influential.

- Conversely, competitive behavior among members of the senior team and their competitive assumptions about others are two of the main reasons why cooperation fails to develop and the Big Freeze takes over.

- The cooperative mindset is fragile; there are a host of attitudes and barriers that can destroy it and degrade cooperative skills.

We will look at the impact of leaders in Chapter 7. For now, let us take a closer look at the system of practices and processes that shape a cooperative mindset. My research into cooperative teams highlighted six practices that play particularly crucial roles.

Practice 1: relational selection. Selection plays a crucial role when it is designed to attract and retain a high proportion of people who are naturally cooperative and shield the company from too many naturally uncooperative and highly competitive people.

Practice 2: relational induction. Induction practices can be important because within the first six weeks of joining a company or starting a job, the socialization process is well under way, and norms of behavior are beginning to emerge. Where a cooperative mindset emerges, induction focusing on building strong, positive relationships is crucial.

Practice 3: mentoring. Cooperative executive behavior provides a role model for cooperative working. Perhaps the most obvious cooperative role an executive can model is actively mentoring others. My research showed that executive mentoring has a profoundly positive impact on the emergence of a cooperative mindset.

Practice 4: collective rewards. Individualized, highly competitive rewards act as a strong disincentive to the emergence of a cooperative mindset. It is clear from the research into Hot Spots that team-based collective rewards do not of themselves encourage cooperation. However, they do have the effect of removing the barrier erected by individualized rewards. In a sense, they are neutral rather than positive.

Practice 5: peer-to-peer working. A mindset of cooperation emerges when there is a sense of mutuality, when people realize that only through working with others will they flourish. Organizational structures that encourage peer-to-peer working serve to support the emergence of this sense of mutuality by developing the habits of working with others.

Practice 6: social responsibility. This sense of mutuality and of being part of something big and important emerges through the practice of social responsibility. By developing the habit of giving freely and cultivating the joy of giving one's time, people can begin to appreciate the immense potential in cooperative working.

Practice 1: relational selection

Companies in which a cooperative mindset flourishes take particular care in their selection practices. The aim is twofold: to encourage cooperatively minded people to join the company and to shield the company from overly competitive and individualistic people. This dual focus in the selection process is played out with great sophistication at the investment bank Goldman Sachs, which regards the selection process as central to the firm's strategy to create a deeply networked and cooperative workforce.[13]

At Goldman Sachs, a mindset of cooperation is crucial to the success of the firm. Collaboration has always been a core value of this premier investment bank because, in the words of its former CEO Hank Paulson, "Quite simply, none of us is as smart as all of us." The entrenched tradition of cooperation is the foundation of the firm's reputation for excellence in execution. "Everywhere and in every country around the world, people know that when a Goldman Sachs banker walks into the room, all of Goldman Sachs comes with him or her," says Robin Neustein, head of the firm's Private Equity Group. "That, in turn, is the outcome of constant work on maintaining the one-firm identity and the internal challenge to be the best and help each other be the best."

The crisscrossing relationship networks inside and outside Goldman Sachs are fueled by a mindset of cooperation. Over the years, the hiring and promotion systems have evolved to carefully screen out people who are incapable of working cooperatively and to identify those most likely to work in a cooperative manner. In Vice Chairman Bob Steel's opinion, cooperation and collaboration are key: "We collaborate better than anyone else does. We are collaborative, secure people who are comfortable being collaborative. We enjoy affiliation and being part of a team. Even as children in a sandbox, we would have wanted to build a bridge together."

The resources required by the selection process are considerable. By way of illustration, in 2000, the firm recruited 500 graduates and over 1,000 undergraduates, representing around 10 percent of the original pool of 10,500 student applications received. About 5,000 applicants spoke to at least ten members of the firm, and about 2,500 spoke to as many as thirty members of the firm. So collectively, members of Goldman Sachs spent over 100,000 hours in conversations with prospective employees.

The signature process of spotting people who, even as children in a sandbox, want to build a bridge together is what the vast resources of Goldman Sachs are focused on. To be involved in the hiring process bestows both the honor and the responsibility for stewarding the company in terms of its human capital. Some of the many thousands of high-potential people who apply to join Goldman Sachs will emerge as superstars. This is how former Chief Operating Officer John Thain describes the firm's attitude toward these potential stars: "People who are not good at working in teams, even if they are individually very good, tend not to do as well here. So the idea that 'I'm a superstar by myself, but I can't work with other people'—that tends to be quite a big career negative" at Goldman Sachs.

The same rigor and focus that go into the selection of graduates is reflected in the process of promotion to partnership. Participating managing directors are selected by the Management Committee on a biannual basis through a rigorous, time- and people-intensive process. Throughout the assessment for promotion, attention is given to evaluating both the commercial acumen of the person in question and the extent to which the candidate is a "culture carrier" for the company.

Practice 2: relational induction

Many of our habits and norms of behavior begin to be formed within the first few weeks of beginning a new job or joining a new company. It is during this time that we are particularly sensitive to the cues around us and to the prevailing norms of behavior. Induction can be a haphazard affair, or it can be a brief introduction to immediate colleagues. In organizations with a strong cooperative mindset newcomers are rapidly introduced to people both inside and, even more important, outside their team. At the same time, they are rapidly socialized into the habits of cooperation within and across groups. At Nokia, this is a key process that supports the emergence of a cooperative mindset.

When a newcomer joins Nokia or takes on a new role, a well-established induction practice takes place. It is strikingly simple but also strikingly effective. Within the first few weeks, the manager formally introduces the new employee to six people within the team and to six people outside the team. This has two important effects on the emergence of a cooperative mindset. First, it kick-starts the development of the relationships that begin to support this cooperative working and begins the development of trust. Next, it legitimizes and encourages cooperation with those beyond the immediate team and by doing so creates the context for the emergence of generalized trust. Even within weeks of joining Nokia or taking a new role, people begin to forge cooperative relationships with others within and outside their groups.

Practice 3: mentoring

We discovered that those teams with a strong, shared mindset of cooperation are more likely to contain a high proportion of team members who have had positive experiences of being mentored. In some cases, they have participated in mentoring schemes. Many had simply had the joy of working with team leaders and executives who actively supported them and their development. These special mentoring relationships have a profound impact on the cooperative mindset. An executive who mentors a younger member of the company is serving as a crucial role model of support and care.

Practice 4: collective rewards

Performance management and rewards are particularly crucial to the emergence of a cooperative mindset. For cooperation to emerge, the barriers erected by highly individualized rewards and bonuses have to be removed. As you have seen, performance management and reward practices that are essentially individualistic and competitive do much to destroy the possibility that a mindset of cooperation will emerge. This is particularly the case for performance management. When an organization is built on an assumption of competition rather than cooperation, performance management becomes essentially a means of monitoring and checking individual performance. When cooperation is the norm, performance management is less about checking and more about feedback. In fact, it could be argued that is impossible to use performance metrics to check, test, and measure whether cooperative working has taken place. This is because the possible extent of cooperation is invisible.

Let me give you an example. Imagine that I am in a situation where it is important that I cooperate with others to succeed. How can my company measure this cooperation? Many of my cooperative acts will be spontaneous and ad hoc. This is particularly the case for cooperation across boundaries. So the first challenge of measuring cooperation is that the potential locus of cooperative relationships is very wide. The second challenge is calculating the extent of my cooperation. My potential for cooperation and engagement in innovation and knowledge sharing is essentially unknowable to others. It may appear that I am cooperating, but what if I am simply going through the motions and am in fact withholding important knowledge? Clearly, it is impossible for the extent of my cooperation to be known, reliably measured, or rewarded.

Does this mean that we should abandon performance management and performance-related pay? I believe that this is a crucial issue for organizations and an area where we really need to be more innovative and thoughtful.

Here are a couple of thoughts. First, if cooperation is relational, then we need to pick up the depth, quality, and extent of relationships when we measure performance. This makes a strong case for 360-degree feedback, in which the views of peers inside and outside a group are actively elicited. Next, if the emergence of a cooperative mindset rests on trust and reciprocity, we have to be particularly vigilant about the potential negative impact on trust that draconian performance measurement systems may have. In essence, performance management should be seen more as a feedback mechanism and less as measurement device. Finally, we need a point of view about remuneration. It is clear that highly individualized bonuses can destroy a cooperative mindset. When people are pitted against each other, their motivation is to compete rather than to cooperate. So is the key to the emergence of a cooperative mindset the development of team-based rewards?

My research shows clearly that reward systems, even team-based reward systems, do not in and of themselves encourage cooperative working. However, team-based rewards do have the important effect of removing the barrier that highly individualized rewards pose to cooperative working.

Over a decade of research has shown that people do not cooperate to obtain rewards for doing so.[14] Too many executives overemphasize the impact of remuneration practices on the behavior of their employees. In fact, there is strong evidence that rewarding cooperation may actually shift the axis of cooperation from a relational exchange to a transactional exchange. Removing the element of individual giving actually destroys some of the joy that people derive from cooperation.[15]

It would be a mistake to place rewards at the center of a strategy to support the emergence of a cooperative mindset. Selection, induction, and leadership behaviors and attitudes are the key points of leverage. Yet at the same time, we must be sensitive to the potentially negative effect rewards can have and work to reduce this potential barrier. At Goldman Sachs, for example, the focus of human resource practices is on the selection of cooperative people. This is the firm's signature process and a practice toward which much executive time and resources are devoted. But even though selection is the primary lever for cooperative working, much thought has gone into rewards and bonus arrangements in the firm. Before the firm became a publicly traded company, each partner was allotted a fixed proportion of whatever the income for the year might be, with no discretionary payment based on any aspect of performance by the partner or the unit. Once Goldman Sachs became a public company, the link between overall firm performance and each partner's compensation was still important, although 60 percent rather than 100 percent of the rewards are now based on the performance of the business unit.

Practice 5: peer-to-peer working

Where a mindset of cooperation emerged, I discovered many examples of peer-to-peer working. These are important because they encourage a sense of cooperation and mutuality. In situations where people work a great deal on their own and are dependent only on their own competencies and skills, it is more difficult for them to develop a sense of trust in others and for a mindset of cooperation to emerge. One of the main ways this sense of mutuality is developed is through practices and processes that allow people to discover and understand that their interests coincide with the interests of others. In these situations, people are encouraged to learn the goals of others and to acknowledge and respect the differences between people. Peer-to-peer practices such as group projects and communities of practice encourage this sense of mutuality and knowledge exchange. Chapter 4 takes a closer look at how peer-to-peer relationships can play a role in developing the sense of trust and mutuality of cooperative working.

Executives can foster mutuality by deepening people's understanding and awareness of the world as others view it. Processes such as brainstorming provide a context where people and ideas can come together to forge a common perspective, avoiding the risks of premature criticism and closure. Other organizational practices, such as regular job rotations and assignments to different parts of the organization, can similarly be used to enrich people's experience of and respect for different perspectives.

Practice 6: social responsibility

The executives in companies where a mindset of cooperation flourishes often practice cooperation both on and off the job. They do this by encouraging and supporting employees' involvement in activities to benefit the wider community. This sort of social responsibility develops the habit of mutuality and teaches that to support and help others is important. Social responsibility activities can also do much to further what Aristotle called moral excellence, a valuable fuel for Hot Spots. The practice of social responsibility can be as simple as the practice of Citigroup's executives when they travel to business meetings. Instead of devoting all their time together to business presentations and discussions, they allocate some of their time to the community in which they are meeting. For example, if the executive team is meeting in central London, members spend half a day in the local community working with disadvantaged youngsters. This has the effect of both building strong relationships within the executive team and modeling the type of mutuality so essential to cooperative groups.

Norms of Trust and Reciprocity Emerge

The norms of trust and reciprocity play a crucial role in the emergence of a cooperative mindset. What are they, and how do they emerge? Let us take a short detour to the streets of New York and follow in the footsteps of the scholar Brian Uzzi.

A short detour to the streets of New York

Brian Uzzi studied the network of friendships and relationships that criss-cross the garment industry of New York City.[16] The city has no single large company designing and manufacturing clothes. Instead, a handful of small companies specialize in cutting the cloth, while other specialist firms make buttonholes and sew on buttons. Other firms assemble the clothes, and others still bring the finished garments to market. The New York garment industry thus consists of many hundreds of small companies that together have created a Hot Spot of innovation and design and a place of deep cooperation.

Uzzi's interest is what holds these small companies together and how the norms of trust and reciprocity emerged over time. How is it that they are able to work so closely together to get ideas to market with such speed and dexterity? In conversation with the garment manufacturers, he heard many stories of how they helped each other out. If one merchant was experiencing a cash flow problem, it was not unusual for another to hold back an invoice for a week or so. A cloth supplier was prepared to deliver material without expecting the manufacturer to pay immediately. Uzzi heard of designers sending out ideas knowing that they would not be illegally copied. Uzzi's expectation was that there would be multiple written contracts describing what each party was agreeing to and the consequences of failure to perform. To his surprise, he found that very few such contracts existed. Like the relationships that Toyota has with its first- and second-tier suppliers, the transactions between the New York garment suppliers, manufacturers, and buyers was more likely to be sealed not with a formal document but with a shake of the hand.

What Brian Uzzi had observed in the garment district of New York is similar to my observations of Hot Spots: that *high-quality relationships* are the conduit for business to be done.[17]

As Uzzi studied these relationships more closely, he found that many went back years, during which time both parties had gotten to know each other and to assess each other's trustworthiness. Those who were not believed to be trustworthy simply did not get the same amount of flexibility as those who were. When people knew each other well over a period of time, they were able to gauge the others' trustworthiness and act on this information. This led Uzzi to wonder whether the length of the relationship between the manufacturers would predict the extent of trust between them. However, he found that this was not a reliable measure, as there were occasions when the small companies worked cooperatively with others whom they did not know particularly well. In such circumstances, a sort of *generalized trust* was operating. Simply put, although one merchant might not know the other directly, they had mutual friends and acquaintances that vouched for them. These reciprocity networks, as he termed them, created general feelings of trust across many parts of the community of manufacturers.

The willingness to cooperate depends to a significant extent on the personal relationships people develop with each other. These relationships shape both the accessibility and the motivation of people to engage with each other in knowledge and learning. My colleagues Janine Nahapiet and Sumantra Ghoshal suggest that four features are especially important influences on cooperation: trust, norms, identification, and obligation (or what I will later term commitments).[18] Where relationships are high in trust, people are more willing to engage in social exchange in general and to be cooperative. In the context of knowledge exchange, trust leads to the openness, dialogue, and the shared experimentation that is so important for innovation.

The garment manufacturers of New York can give us some insight into the nature of cooperation and the importance of high-quality relationships. However, in understanding Uzzi's study, we must remember that the garment district of Manhattan has a number of important attributes. First, it is proximate: perhaps half a mile from one end to the other. So as they walk around the streets of the district, the merchants are continuously meeting with each other, having conversations, and exchanging information. Pertti at Nokia or Polly at BP do not have the luxury of proximity. They will need to cooperate with people at the other end of the world. Not only are the garment merchants of New York arrayed close to each other, but as noted, in many cases, they have known each other for many years, during which time they have had the opportunity to observe the others in a variety of situation and have judged their trustworthiness. In many contemporary companies, innovation and flexibility require people to cooperate at a far earlier stage in their relationships, while they are still strangers. And the garment manufacturers of New York have one additional advantage: they are rather similar. They are all in the same business, most are around the same age, and most are Jewish. These similarities made it relatively easier for a durable sense of generalized trust and reciprocity to develop. As you will learn in Chapter 4, when people are distant, dissimilar, and strangers, the forging of cooperative relationships becomes even more crucial.

CHAPTER SUMMARY

THE FIRST ELEMENT: A COOPERATIVE MINDSET

Key Points

Companies that abound with Hot Spots are smart about using all points of leverage to encourage a mindset of cooperation, including the following:

- Candidate selection practices that prevent the company from hiring overly competitive employees and encourage the selection of cooperative individuals

- Rewarding practices that encourage team rather than individual performance

- Positive executive leadership practices that encourage and model cooperative working

- Mentoring and coaching

- The creation and communication of symbols, stories, and language of cooperation

- Informal activities and events that encourage a sense of mutuality

The New Rules of Cooperation

- **Relationships** The value of Hot Spots is created in the space between people. Hot Spots are fundamentally relational, whether the relationship is between close friends or acquaintances. The new rule is that the focus of resources with regard to support and development needs to be on the individual and on the person's network of relationships.

- **Emergence** Hot Spots emerge on their own; they cannot be ordered forth or directed. People choose freely to give of their human capital (intellectual, emotional, or social)—they volunteer.

4

THE SECOND ELEMENT: BOUNDARY SPANNING

Hot Spots = (Cooperative Mindset x <u>Boundary Spanning</u> x Igniting Purpose) x Productive Capacity

A MINDSET OF COOPERATION is the foundation for the emergence of Hot Spots—and with this the trust and reciprocity that are so vital to Hot Spots. As the relationships within a Hot Spot emerge, they do so in a rather predictable way. Cooperating with friends in the immediate working environment often sets the stage for the birth of a Hot Spot. Yet this is rarely sufficient. When Hot Spots flourish and became productive and innovative, these initial networks of relationships expand from immediate colleagues to stretch across the boundaries of groups, functions, and companies. Amit and his colleagues at Linux are working across the world, connected as volunteers in an endeavor that fills them with passion and creates a shared sense of purpose and intellectual sparkle. Polly and Carlos at BP are engaged in a Hot Spot with relationships and friendships that link Poland and Venezuela in an effort to share knowledge and ideas. Tim and Nigel at OgilvyOne are members of teams that are linking across the boundaries of OgilvyOne and NoHo Digital. Spanning boundaries is critical to the vitality and longevity of a Hot Spot.

Boundary Spanning and Value Creation

Relationships that span boundaries are so critical to the vitality and longevity of a Hot Spot because the value that a Hot Spot creates is produced through both the *exploitation* of the current knowledge of those people within the Hot Spot and the *exploration and novel combinations* of this knowledge. When the network of relationships stretches across boundaries, the variety and range of insights and knowledge are greater than when the network of relationships is within a single group.

Value creation and knowledge

Not all knowledge is of equal value, and the distinctions in types of knowledge have important implications for the means by which productive innovation arises in Hot Spots. The people engaged in a Hot Spot have two kinds of knowledge: explicit and implicit.[1]

Some knowledge is *explicit and objective,* easy to write down and to access. Explicit knowledge moves with ease across the boundaries of a company. Manuals, Web sites, and books enable and support the diffusion of explicit knowledge. Since explicit knowledge is relatively easy to record and communicate, it is able to exist independent of a particular person or group. Recall that in Peter's company, the service engineers had a manual that contained information about how to service the various machines the company produced. At OgilvyOne, the Truffles intranet is simply an electronic library of the explicit knowledge of the people in the firm.

Knowledge can also be *tacit and experiential.* This is knowledge that is built up over time by people and the groups of which they are members. Think of Carlos in BP's business unit in Venezuela. A portion of his understanding of how to create a retail business in a growing market will be tacit knowledge. He and his colleagues have written various project reports that describe their approach and the outcomes. It is likely that a larger proportion of the insight and knowledge of Carlos and his colleagues will be tacit. Since this tacit knowledge is held in their minds and is part of the way they see the world, it is much more difficult than explicit knowledge to express and to codify. As a consequence, manuals and books cannot readily diffuse tacit knowledge. Polly will only really share Carlos's tacit knowledge if she begins to get to know him and if he trusts her. On the streets of New York City, for example, the garment manufacturers have a great deal of shared tacit knowledge about who buys what or how the season is likely to emerge.

So while explicit knowledge typically stands outside the relationships between people, codified in manuals and on Web sites, tacit knowledge is fundamentally based within relationships. In a sense, the tacit knowledge in a Hot Spot becomes the property of that Hot Spot. This tacit knowledge can be an aspect of how the Hot Spot flourishes, of the habits and skills of the participants, and of the routines and practices that the Hot Spot has adopted.

Value creation and relationships

It is clear that the value created in a Hot Spot depends in part on the capacity of the people in the Hot Spot to exchange and combine tacit and explicit knowledge. As you saw in the example of Polly and Carlos, the depth and extent of these relationships are critical. For example, although Carlos does not need to know Polly to share with her the project reports he has prepared, he does need to know her and trust her if he is to share the deep insights and tacit knowledge he has.

In recent years, scholars such as Ron Burt and David Krackhardt have taken a closer look at relationships at work.[2] They distinguish between two broad categories of relationships. Some relationships go back years, are based on trust and reciprocity, and have an emotional element. They call these *strong ties*. Most of us have about three to six strong ties at any point in our lives, with women having significantly more of these close relationships, or strong ties, than men.

Many of the relationships we have at work and outside of work do not have this extent of history, trust, or emotion. These are our acquaintances, people we meet less frequently, with whom we do not have a strong emotional attachment—in short, these are our *weak ties*. We can sustain many more of these weak ties than we can strong ties since they take up less of our time and energy. Some of us may have many thousands of such connections. We devote far more time and emotional resources to maintaining our small network of strong ties than to our larger network of weak ties. Different ties may be active at various times, and what we might think of as *latent ties,* relationships that have been strong in the past but are now dormant, can be rapidly reignited at any point in time.

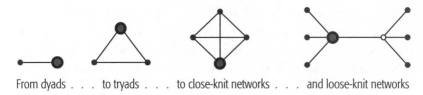

From dyads . . . to tryads . . . to close-knit networks . . . and loose-knit networks

Figure 4.1 The evolution of networks in a Hot Spot

Typically as Hot Spots emerge, the initial dyads of close friends intro-duce other people, and these networks evolve in many different ways, with some close-knit connections and some much looser (see Figure 4.1).

The network ties within a Hot Spot are likely to be very complex, contain-ing strong ties and weak ties that cross group, business, function, company, and country boundaries. Researchers in the field of network theory illustrate the ties within networks by plotting the major ties between people in what is known as a *sociogram*. Figure 4.2 is a sociogram showing the ties between the members of a multiunit business. These only include the ties *within* the business. If we included those outside, the drawing would be even more com-plex. The lines in the diagram plot who knows whom, with the people in the center having the largest number of ties and those at the periphery the smallest number of ties. This particular network illustration is of a family owned com-pany—so some network ties are within the family unit, while other network ties are with people who are not members of the family.

Hot Spots form as the result of an igniting purpose across networks of relationship ties. Hot Spots will contain both strong ties, going back many years and based on mutual respect and reciprocity, and weak ties, no more than acquaintances focused on the same igniting question. The type and extent of these relationship ties have a significant impact on the knowledge flows throughout the Hot Spot and hence on the capacity of the Hot Spot to create value.

To understand this better, let's take a look back at the matrix presented in Figure 1.2, reproduced here as Figure 4.3. The close relationships (strong ties) within a Hot Spot are likely to foster the sharing of tacit knowledge and expertise. Recall that tacit knowledge is typically developed over time and is embedded within the relationships and experiences of a network of people. Tacit knowledge is more likely to be developed in strong ties that have continuity through time. These strong ties create a base of trust that can reduce resistance to sharing knowledge and expertise and provide comfort in the face of uncertainty and ambiguity. Many of these strong

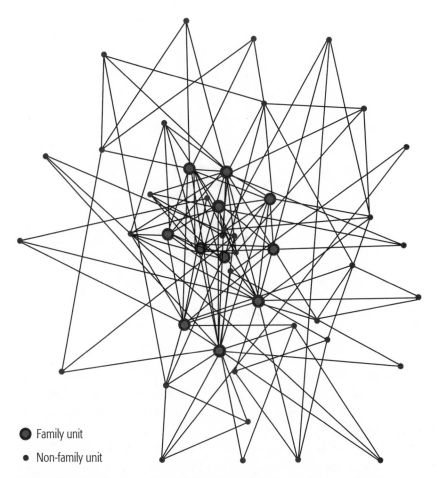

Family unit

Non-family unit

Figure 4.2 A sociogram of the relationships between people in a multiunit company

Source: M. Kilduff and W. Tsai, *Social Networks and Organizations* (Thousand Oaks, Calif.: Sage, 2003), p. 27

ties will be with others in the same group, and these ties are crucial to the exploitation of knowledge through shared expertise. However, these strong ties within well-established groups are rarely places where innovative value is created.

The creation of value from new ideas and innovation typically requires a rather different evolution of the ties within a Hot Spot. In the 1970s, 1980s, and 1990s, various scholars showed why networks and ties are so important to the innovative capacity of companies such as BP, Nokia, and OgilvyOne.[3] What they learned was profoundly counterintuitive and profoundly important. One might have anticipated that the best ideas and

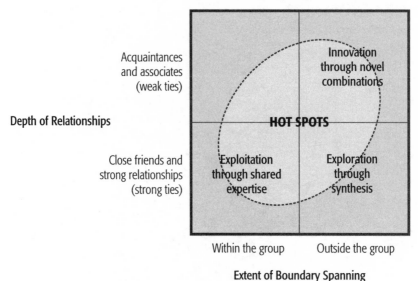

Figure 4.3 Effects of relationship quality on value creation in Hot Spots

innovations arise from relationships that go back a long time, through strong ties—in other words, from people who know each other, trust each other, and find it easy and straightforward to cooperate with each other. This makes intuitive sense.

But it is wrong. In fact, the researchers found that although these work groups crisscrossed with strong ties can be excellent at surfacing known tacit knowledge, they are generally poor at creating new ideas and innovation. The reason turns out to be quite simple: in relationships with strong ties, people talk about what they already know, and since there is much overlap among them, there is much redundancy of knowledge.

The truth is that new ideas and insights usually come not from strong ties but rather from the many weak ties that people have. So Carlos, with all his experience in Venezuela, and Polly, with her experience in the United States and Poland, are linked by precisely the sort of weak ties that have the potential to stimulate new ideas and innovation.

Value can thus be created within the networks of a Hot Spot in three ways, corresponding to the quadrants of Figure 4.3:

- **Value through exploitation.** Where there are many *strong ties within a group*—the lower left quadrant of Figure 4.3—members of the group are particularly adept at maintaining and exploiting the tacit knowledge possessed by members of the group. They have worked together over time, know each other well, and see each other frequently. These are the experts—the guardians of the knowledge of the firm.

- **Value through innovation.** Where there are a large number of *weak ties* (acquaintances and associates) that *cross boundaries*—the upper right quadrant—information is diffused faster and is made available to a larger number of people. Here there is potential to create value through dynamic new combinations and access to novel information.

- **Value through exploration.** Where there are *strong ties* that *cross boundaries*—the lower right quadrant—there is potential of new ideas arising through the combination of what is known by people across the boundaries. They know each other well and can explore what each other knows, with the potential of synthesis.

What is clear from this research on innovation is that boundaries are very important to the creation of value through novel combinations. Crossing boundaries is crucial to Hot Spots. Let us take a closer look at what these boundaries can be.

Boundaries

Hot Spot networks that cross boundaries are rich sources of potential value creation through exploration and innovation. Over the past century, the boundaries that separate people within and across companies have become ever more complex as the structure of companies has changed. One of the major changes in these boundaries has come with the adoption of the divisional structure, the creation of separate business units. Typically, these divisions represent a major product line, with their own separate R&D, production, marketing, and sales departments. The advantages of this fragmentation are powerful. The structure enables companies to move rapidly into new markets and develop new product lines merely through the addition of a new division.[4]

With this management innovation came ever more complex boundaries. What this means for the emergence of Hot Spots is that the complexity of the boundaries between people had risen exponentially. What had historically been craft-based workers collaborating on the creation of a single product has become a mass of complex boundaries between one function and another and between one business unit and another. The complexity was not to end there. In the Ford Motor Company of the early 1900s, for example, most of the value of the company was created within the boundaries of the company. Leather seats were sewn, engine shafts were molded, and even tires were produced within the company. Starting in the 1940s, companies began to move production of some components to suppliers based outside the company. As this trend gathered speed, more and more of the value of a company was created outside of its formal boundaries.

The work within the boundaries had also changed, as Figure 4.4 illustrates. Historically, much of the work in companies was performed in formal work groups. However, over the past decade or so, an increasing proportion of work is performed in project teams and task forces. You will see later how Nokia, for example, makes extensive of task forces and project teams. Some of these task forces are directed, but many are emergent, with people volunteering to join them. This emergent volunteerism is particularly apparent in communities of practice and creativity. These are communities powered less by the needs of a specific task or problem and more by shared passion. The community of Linux is essentially a community of creativity with shared knowledge and passion.

Boundaries across communities of practice

Polly and Carlos at BP, Pertti at Nokia, and Nigel and Tim at OgilvyOne are all members of a company but are also members of a community of practice.[5] Talk to Nigel about his interest and passion, and he will tell you about the network he maintains with people who are also in the advertising industry. The same is true for Pertti. He is a member of a Hot Spot that has emerged around a community of practice of people fascinated with video telephony. Members from across the world and spanning companies and research institutions share this common passion. These Hot Spots around communities of practice typically evolve in the way shown in Figure 4.1. They begin as dyadic relationships—in this case, Pertti met an assistant professor called Simon at a conference at a U.S. engineering school. Over time, Simon introduced Pertti to his colleagues with a similar interest. They had begun to "invent" activities to work on together. The intellectual sparkle between them had become the kernel of a Hot Spot.

Their first invented activity arose when Simon spent a couple of weeks with Pertti's Nokia team, informally discussing shared interests. This resulted in Pertti's sponsoring two of Simon's doctoral students and intro-

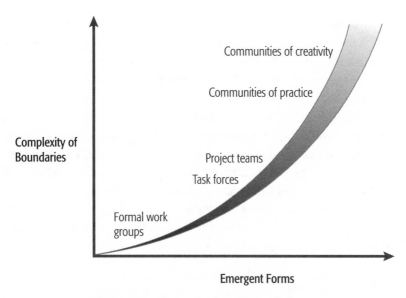

Figure 4.4 The expansion of boundaries

ducing Simon and his colleagues to the internal network of practitioners within Nokia. Over time, a Hot Spot had begun to emerge that is of real value to Simon and Pertti in terms of their own development and also in terms of their potential to add value to the wider working communities of which they are members.

Communities of practice are unlike formal work groups, project teams, or task forces, which typically have formally defined goals and an explicit agenda. Instead these are much looser groupings of people who have a great deal of shared knowledge and overlapping ways of looking at the world.

Boundaries across communities of creativity

The Hot Spots in communities of practice are places where ideas and knowledge are shared. When they become places where tasks are performed, they become communities of creativity. This is ultimately what Linux is. Amit has not been formally contracted to work at Linux; he has no employment contract. Amit is a volunteer. As such, he and other Linux workers do not conform to many of our assumptions about why and how people work. He does not receive monetary compensation for his labors, and he does not have a job description or performance reviews. Contributing to Linux is a choice that he has personally made, of his own volition and free will. In this sense, Amit and his Linux colleagues support and reinforce founder Linus Torvalds's mission: "I generally don't ask people to do anything special. I want people to work on projects because they want to work on them, not because they feel they should. That's how you motivate good morale and code quality."[6]

The Hot Spots that flare up across the Linux community are emergent. They are not designed from a strategic document, nor do senior executives prescribe them. Rather these Hot Spots emerge as a result of the interests and passions of the people who freely choose to join the Linux community. These Hot Spots are shaped by the day-to-day problems that crop up in the course of the maintenance and development of the Linux system.

If the value created within Hot Spots arises from across these boundaries, then this leaves us with a number of crucial questions:

- How do people across the boundaries of a Hot Spot learn to cooperate with each other when they are potentially so different?

- What experiences, skills, and competencies support the capacity to be a boundary spanner?

- What role, if any, can executives play in supporting and enabling boundary spanning?

◙ Learning to Cooperate Across Boundaries

Here is the paradox: we know that value—from exploitation of knowledge and innovation through new combinations—is most likely to be created across boundaries. We also know that working across boundaries is challenging. Let me illustrate this with the data from my Hot Spot research. In this research, my colleagues and I studied more than fifty groups in seventeen companies. We collected data from team members, team leaders, and business unit heads. What we discovered was that groups that cooperated with each other and shared knowledge between them are more productive. However, when we took a closer look at the complexity of the groups— with regard to the distance between members and the degree of diversity within the group (in terms of nationality, experience and age)—we found that many of these complex and diverse groups were less productive. I have illustrated the distribution of the performance of the groups in Figure 4.5, where each dot represents a group. As this distribution shows, many of the highly cooperative and productive groups are also of low complexity—they

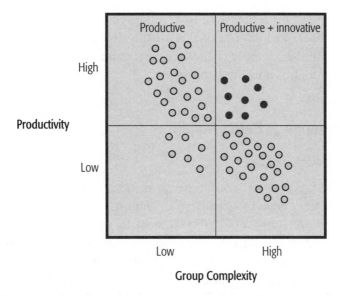

Figure 4.5 The relationship between productivity and group complexity

are groups in which people work in the same location and are of a similar age and gender. We also found that many of the productive groups are of high complexity—groups in which people are working virtually and are of different ages and nationalities. However, and this is the crucial point, although the groups in the low-complexity/high-productivity quadrant were indeed productive, they were not particularly innovative. It was the relatively small number of groups in the high-complexity/high-productivity quadrant that were also innovative. This should not surprise us. If you think back to Figure 4.3, we noted that boundary spanning fuels innovation through novel combinations. These high-complexity groups were populated by people from different functions, businesses, and age groups. In other words, they were rich in boundaries.

Learning to cooperate across boundaries is tough, but the prize is innovation. The likelihood is that these complex groups will be unproductive, yet some manage to leap across the barriers of complexity. To do so they have to face three challenges.

The first challenge is distance: how can people work cooperatively with other across vast distances and time zones? The second challenge is difference: how can people work cooperatively across boundaries with people very different from themselves? The third challenge is unfamiliarity: how can people work cooperatively with others who are mere acquaintances or even strangers? This is the paradox: that the very aspects that create value in a Hot Spot are also the aspects that are the most challenging. And yet in successful Hot Spots, these challenges are met and value is created. Let's take a closer look at how this happens.

Challenge 1: Being Distant

The power of proximity

Imagine that it is your first week at college. You have come alone and now live in the dorm. Over the coming years, you will form friendships, some of which will last for the rest of your life. Who will these friends be? Where will natural Hot Spots develop? You have the many thousands of students at the college to choose from, and some, like yourself, will be first-year students.

Psychologists have asked this very same question and have answered it by plotting the extent and depth of the networks of friendships that individual students develop over their first year at college. Given the many choices these students have to make friends, one might predict that the students will form networks of friendships with people from all parts of the college. But this is rarely the case. Instead, the probability is that the closest and longest-lasting friendships will be formed with students rooming in the adjacent dorms.[7] In fact, there is a clear correlation between degree of friendship and dorm distance. The closer the dorm, the greater the likelihood of a positive relationship.

The students in this research are not particularly unusual in their choice of friends. Study after study has shown that ultimately each one of us tends to form relationships with and to trust the people whom we see a great deal of. And we are more likely to see a great deal of some people simply because they are located near us. We bump into them in the corridor, we begin to talk with them about themselves, we learn we have something in common, we talk more about our shared interests—before we know it, we are friends. Of course, there are occasions when the converse is true, when as we see more and more of certain people, we like them less and less. But most of the time, being located near someone and therefore spending time with them increases our positive feelings toward them. There is little empirical support for the adage that familiarity breeds contempt.

So the first challenge of Hot Spots is the challenge of distance. Proximity is powerful. The challenge is that many of the members in a Hot Spot will not be proximate. Think back to Pertti at Nokia and the challenges he and his colleagues face in the Chinese market.

The challenge of time zones

Being distant can also involve working across different time zones. This challenge is subtle but profound. Take a notion as simple as "coffee time." When people are located in the same time zone, they can use "coffee time" as a time for informal connection. Think back to how many times in the last month you have said to a friend or acquaintance, "Let's meet for coffee and talk about this" or "I'll phone you during your coffee break." Very little else needs to be said. These connections are informal, flexible, and outside the tight scheduling of time. Most cultures have a concept of when a coffee break is appropriate and how long a meeting over coffee will last. Now consider Pertti's challenge in the Hot Spot he is creating at Nokia with his Asian colleagues. There is no possibility of his casually saying to his Chinese colleagues, "Let's meet at coffee time and talk more about this." They are not in the same location or even at the same point in their day, so this type of chance encounter is an impossibility, and there is no shared notion of coffee time. In Hot Spots that span time zones, as many do, the casualness of shared time-based rituals like coffee time is not available.

This presents a significant challenge for the emergence of Hot Spots. For a great deal of the history of humans and cooperative working, people were able to make use of place and time as major coordinating principles. When, for example, the tradesmen of the fourteenth century decided to work together, they simply used the center of the town as the place of meeting. Without access to accurate chronological time, their cooperation was dependent on space and place. They agreed to meet in a certain place at an approximate time of the day, and that place and that space acted as the means of coordination. Without the place and the space, there would be no means for them to come together in a predictable manner. Working together followed the ebb and flow of the day and the seasons.

With the invention of the mechanical clock, tradesmen no longer needed to use space as a coordinator. They no longer needed to come together in the square of the town to meet. In fact, it was possible for them to coordinate their meetings beforehand simply by specifying the time to meet. In recent centuries, clock time has become more and more central to the way we cooperate. It bounds the present time, the time we meet, and the time we complete our meetings. Clock time creates a boundary for future time, through schedules and plans. The timetables we create are able to fix us in time and in space; they have become a means by which we order our day.

So here is the dilemma: to create sophisticated coordination practices to span time zones may well be sensible; however, doing so may also have a significant negative impact on the lightness and adaptability that give rise to the most productive Hot Spots.

The challenge of time in Hot Spots is that this overreliance on schedules and measuring time can have a profoundly negative impact on Hot Spots. Creativity and innovation suffer when time is viewed as money, as a limited resource. People in Hot Spots suffer from stress and anxiety when there is an overemphasis on the compression of time, when the overwhelming agenda is to put as much as possible into the time we have, where excess time is viewed as "slack."

Leaping across distance

So how do people in successful Hot Spots meet the challenge of distance? For one thing, they typically make use of a whole host of socialization practices that ensure that people learn as much as possible about each other at the very beginning of the Hot Spot. The relational induction we explored in Chapter 3 is important to leaping across distances, and in Chapter 6, we take a closer look at the practice of appreciating talents.

They also use technology to create what we might call "intimacy across space." The Truffles technology at OgilvyOne, for example, creates an important link between the employees of the company who are located across the world.

Challenge 2: Being Different

Like the challenge of distance, the challenge of difference was discovered through experiments in psychology. Just as first-year college students are likely to form a positive relationship with the person in the next room, so too are they more likely to form a positive relationship with someone who is like them. Decisions about similarity are made in the blink of an eye.

The power of similarity

In a fascinating series of studies, psychologists asked students to rate how positively they felt about the people they were shown in a series of photographs, people whom the students had never met. In the first part of the study, students were shown pictures of people and asked to rate their positive feelings toward each person. Next, a group of researchers rated the similarity between the faces of the students and the faces of the persons they rated. The results were astounding. In the vast majority of cases, there was a high correlation between the two ratings. The more similar the face of the student and the picture they were shown, the more positive the student's response. Taken to its extremes, psychologists have also reported that in choosing a partner, we are more likely to be attracted to and ultimately to marry people with features similar to our own.[8]

The implications of these studies for Hot Spots are profound. Let's go back to the room in Helsinki. In the afternoon gloom, the video flickers on to reveal the face of Pertti's Chinese colleague, Huang who works in Nokia's Beijing office. Psychologists observing the scene would predict that in the blink of an eye, the Finns around the table in Helsinki would be slightly wary of Huang and his colleagues. This is before Huang has even opened his mouth. If Pertti and his Finnish colleagues are feeling rather wary, they are simply following the human instinct to be more positive about people who look the same as they do. That is not of course to say that this will be the case for everyone gathered in the room. It may be that Pertti and his colleagues have lived in Asia, and proximity and familiarity have overridden similarity. It could be that they have been taught intercultural sensitivity and have learned the habits of cooperating with people who are different from them. However, for many people, the initial reaction will be neutral or possibly even negative.

Indeed, first perceptions are often negative, and in many cases, they are likely to persist. Psychologists studying multicultural teams have found that the interactions between members of the team differ markedly over time. At a very early stage in a multicultural meeting, an implicit "pecking order" of status is established. Within minutes, the highest-status members (often white males) will take up more of the group's time and establish more positive relationships with those whom they judge to be most like them. As the meeting progresses, psychologists have observed, the contribution of lower-status team members (for example, Asian females) rapidly diminishes.

Cross-cultural differences

Cooperation across country boundaries brings even more subtle challenges than distance and difference. When Pertti and Huang are videoconferencing, they are speaking as individuals but also as a Finn and a Chinese. Anyone with experience with multicultural teams can predict that there will be important and profound cultural differences between these citizens of different countries. What's more, these differences may well have a crucial negative impact on the likelihood of their being able to cooperate and to ignite a Hot Spot. The differences can be very subtle, but they are nevertheless profoundly important.

Take the attitude we have toward others and the responsibilities we feel for others. These are important concerns because they influence the type and extent of relationships in Hot Spots. Research on national differences has shown there are strong differences between people in various countries and regions in terms of their attitudes toward others. Some countries, particularly Asian countries, are more collectivistic; people in these countries are more likely to take account of the needs and wishes of others and will go to great lengths to remain part of the community. In Huang's Chinese culture, a person is defined in terms of one's relation to other people. His is essentially a relational culture.[9] By contrast, the people in most Western countries are more autonomous. They are more likely to put themselves rather than the team first, and they are less concerned with staying within the community. In the Western culture that Pertti comes from, which is essentially individualistic, the self is defined as a self-contained entity, with each person seen as autonomous and independent from others. However, we should note that this is not true to the same extent in all Western countries. Pertti, a Finn, will have a different set of assumptions from Tim and Nigel in the United Kingdom, since Finland has one of the most collectivist outlooks of the Western countries.

Personality differences

Each of us has our own unique personality. Bridging to others inevitably means working cooperatively with people who are not the same as us. Nowhere is this more potentially challenging than in personality differences regarding time and pacing. Recall that one aspect of the challenge of distance is the potential difficulty of working across time zones. As we noted, Hot Spots, and the social connectivity within them, are time-dependent.[10] Meetings are scheduled, tasks are planned, and the ebb and flow of the Hot Spot evolves. Time zones present potential difficulties for Hot Spots, and differences in personality types can do the same. I have found that often when Hot Spots cool down, conflicts and ambiguity about time are among the key contributing factors. When Hot Spots failed, I heard people say how difficult they found working with each other—not because they were not in the same room or even because they were different but because they wanted to work at a different pace. Some members believed their counterparts were too fast and superficial, and others thought the group was too slow and ponderous.

Much of this difference in time preference is a reflection of the so-called Type A personality. For Type A people, time urgency is crucial.[11] They are likely to pay a great deal of attention to the passage of time. They constantly check the time remaining and see time as their enemy. In fact, researchers have shown that time-urgent people tend to schedule more activities than can comfortably fit into the available time. So they become chronically hurried, trying to fulfill all of their ambitions and commitments under unrealistic deadline situations that they themselves have created. So when time-urgent people become involved in Hot Spots, to complete all the activities they have scheduled, they are likely to be very efficient in their use of time. Typically, they will use deadlines to prioritize tasks, become preoccupied with deadlines, and therefore increase their work pace. These Type A characters are important to Hot Spots—they have the potential to keep things moving and active.

However, the urgency of Type A characters can also have a detrimental impact on the Hot Spot. This can occur even in Hot Spots where people all work in the same location and seem personally quite similar. Take Tim at NoHo Digital, for example. Tim started his life as a creative software developer. It could be that he is a non-time-urgent individual. So as the Hot Spot around the merger of the two companies develops, Tim may well be less attentive to the remaining time resources and to underestimate the passage of time. Clearly, if he is faced with a tight schedule, this underestimation of the passage of time may prove costly, for he may ignore or miss important deadlines. However, adopting an increased pace may prove difficult for non-time-urgent individuals such as Tim.[12]

So what happens when Type A and less time-urgent people get to work together? A team of psychologists from the University of Illinois replicated exactly this situation.[13] They looked specifically at teams who were responsible for completing creative tasks. They found that under these conditions, Type A, time-urgent people reduced the innovative performance of the team because they tended to impose strict, linear schedules on team members, pushing them to focus on one primary task at a time and constantly warning about the time remaining to complete the task. When time is compressed, collaborators typically become more anxious. Of course, a certain level of anxiety has a positive impact on the ability to work productively, but too much anxiety interferes with the ability to focus on complex cognitive tasks. In short, under time pressure and increased anxiety, we freeze. And when this happens, we fall back on information we already know rather than exploring new ways of solving the problem. Often this known information is not the most optimal way of looking at the problem. So instead of looking carefully and rationally at the issue, we rapidly engage with heuristics. These heuristics are the mental models we have of the world. Most of the time, these heuristics help us process information in a complex environment. However, when a community uses heuristics as the primary way of looking at problems, the group can end up adopting suboptimal and significantly less creative solutions.

So even though Type A characters can push Hot Spots along, this can work to the detriment of the creativity and insight of the Hot Spot. If there are too many time-urgent people in a Hot Spot, it is likely to burn itself out.[14]

In part, these differences in time orientation arise from differences in our personalities. However, there are also well-documented cultural differences in time orientation. Take America and China, for example. Scholars such as Tim Hall believe that American and Chinese perceptions of time are mirror images.[15] Americans are more likely to engage in several activities at the same time. In Eastern cultures, the preference is to focus on one thing at a time. As Hot Spots emerge, fundamental cognitive, behavioral, and cultural differences between people can become sources of misunderstanding, conflict, and inconsistency.

Bridging differences

In successful Hot Spots, the barrier of difference can be surmounted in a number of ways:

- By creating a wide degree of flexibility that enables people to work at their own pace and yet with sufficient synchronization that their efforts can be pulled together (Chapter 6 takes a closer look at the practice of synchronizing time.)

- By providing feedback on progress so that mutual adjustments can be made to coordinate across time and space.

- By intertwining action-based work with times of reflection so that participants in a Hot Spot experience periods of time pressure interspersed with times for reflection and playfulness (Chapter 6 takes a closer look at the practices of creating rhythm and supporting timelessness.)

Challenge 3: Being Strangers

Productive and creative Hot Spots often extend to individuals and groups who started out as strangers. Typically, these strangers are members of in-groups of their own. When Hot Spots cross the boundaries of groups, the aspect of in-group and out-group status can posse a threat to its capacity to create value.

In-groups and out-groups

As the members of a group forge a stronger sense of shared identity, they come to see themselves as the in-group and everyone else as the out-group. Over time, this identity strengthens around what is deemed right and appropriate. So over time, this shared identity accentuates similarities within the group. Members of the group become more alike, and the people in other groups become more different, with their differences being accentuated over time.[16] Knowing a lot about one's own group and little about the other group sets the process of stereotyping in motion. People in the in-group begin to accentuate one or two characteristics of members of the other group: "they're all eggheads"; "they don't live in the real world"; "they're all aggressive and competitive."[17] This stereotyping is the beginning of turf battles between the businesses of a company and is the basis of what I call the "silo mentality." In a silo mentality each group, function or business develops increasingly impermeable boundaries between itself and others. People don't move out of the silo and strangers are not accepted within it.

My colleagues and I began to catch a glimpse of this during the merger of NoHo Digital and OgilvyOne. At one point, Tim commented to Nigel, "Some of the creative types at NoHo Digital see this merger like David and Goliath. They hate what big advertising agencies like OgilvyOne and its owner, WPP, stand for. They joined a young start-up to get away from big companies, and now they find themselves being swallowed up by one!" Tim is part of an in-group at NoHo Digital that has strong (and probably stereotypical) views about the out-group at OgilvyOne. In fact, of course, all people at both OgilvyOne and NoHo Digital have much in common. Many are about the same age, are of the same nationality, have chosen to work in a creative profession, and live in London. Yet despite these similarities, they believe their values and beliefs to be fundamentally different. Both companies are places where in-groups have formed.

To understand how this might have occurred, let's return for a moment to the self-fulfilling prophecy discussed in Chapter 3 and illustrated in

Figure 3.1. At OgilvyOne, employees joined the company because of what it stood for. They then selected others into the company and mentored, coached, and socialized each other. Inevitably, over time, they became more and more like each other. A rather different process of selection, socialization, and development occurred at NoHo Digital. As a consequence, each group formed its own closely knit team with its own sense of identity, its own language, and its own norms. The behavior of group members became more and more similar, and their attitudes came more into alignment over time. Simply put, they identified more and more with each other. As people identify more and more with members of their own group, they identify less and less with members of other groups. Their own sense of collective identity grows, and that serves to strengthen the boundaries between them and others.

So for Tim and Nigel, cooperating across this boundary and potentially forming a Hot Spot will not be simply about replicating some of the old ways. Similarly, the old way of managing Finnish technicians in Helsinki is not going to work for Pertti. He is doomed if he assumes homogeneity in a world that is ever more diverse. In each of these situations, Hot Spots crossed boundaries separating people who are strikingly similar to each other from those strikingly different. To achieve this, participants in Hot Spots had to become less like strangers by breaking down the boundaries between in-groups and out-groups.

Becoming less like a stranger

Some of the most creative and innovative Hot Spots are filled with people from very different places, with their own separate identities, who have found a way of working with each other. How have they achieved this? Every Hot Spot emerges along its own idiosyncratic route; each is in a company with supporting signature processes. Yet all Hot Spots have a number of similarities that help members become less distant, less different, and less like strangers.

Learning to Cooperate Across Boundaries: Becoming Less Distant, Less Different, and Less like Strangers

Many things can separate people across boundaries. In creative, productive Hot Spots, people find ways to become less distant, less different, and less like strangers. Beyond all the practices and processes we have discussed, three appear to be central to boundary spanning:

- **Engaging in purposeful conversation.** Perhaps the most important way in which Hot Spots are able to span boundaries is by having people converse with each other in what I call *purposeful conversation.* As you will see, purposeful conversations can be both bonding conversation and heedful interaction.

- **Valuing boundary spanners.** The walls between in-groups and out-groups are broken down by "boundary spanners." These are people who have a network of relationships that form a natural bridge between the two groups. As you will see later, the real advantage of these boundary spanners is that they are able to explain the groups to each other and to point out what is of common interest. These boundary spanners have particular aspirations and competencies that are particularly suited to this role.

- **Widening the net of involvement.** Hot Spots are most likely to bridge boundaries when the context in which people work encourages them to work across boundaries. Nokia was particularly adept at this, and later in this chapter, we will take a closer look at the practices and processes that developed in the company to widen the net of involvement. We will also take a closer look at Nokia's signature modular structure.

Creating a Hot Spot with people who are on the same team, in the same building, of the same nationality, in the same time zone, with the same sense of time, and of the same frame of mind is relatively straightforward. However, although these groupings may become cozy places for people to work, they may lack the innovation and dynamism of Hot Spots. The people in them are just too similar. Hot Spots become more vibrant and innovative, more potentially productive and exciting, when they span boundaries.

Spanning Boundaries Through Purposeful Conversation

Hot Spots abound with people who competently engage in purposeful conversation. Bonding conversations are particularly crucial to the creation of initial relationships (or what I earlier referred to as weak ties). Later, heedful interaction becomes more important as members of the Hot Spot deal with the day-to-day issues they face.

Bonding conversation

As a Hot Spot emerges, many of the initial conversations are bonding conversations, in which two or sometimes three people start to learn about each other. Take, for example, the conversations that Nigel and Tim had as they worked to merge OgilvyOne and NoHo Digital. Each was pursuing a purpose—to merge their two companies. At the beginning, they knew very little of each other. They had a common body of knowledge; after all, both men had been around the advertising industry for decades. But they did not yet know each other as people. At this early stage, personal chemistry was crucial to the initial decision to merge, but it was no more that that. In the months that followed their first meeting, Nigel and Tim began to build a social relationship; they began to engage in bonding conversation. These bonding conversations are critical in the emergence of the networks we saw in Figure 4.1—initially dyads, then triads, evolving into close-knit networks and then to parts of looser networks.

These bonding conversations allow and encourage relationships to form. For Tim and Nigel at OgilvyOne, one of the important aspects of their bonding conversations was the slow but steady development of trust. This trust began as each attempted to understand the other's character. Tim from NoHo Digital in particular had to learn more about Nigel's integrity, his motives and intentions, the consistency of his behavior, and his openness and discreetness. Nigel in his conversations was doing the same; he too was interested in Tim's character. We might also expect that both would also be judging each other's competence. Tim would be judging whether Nigel can ultimately be trusted to have the competence and skills to move OgilvyOne into the digital age.

Over the months following their initial meeting in London, Nigel and Tim spent much of their time in conversation. Many of these conversations occurred in the offices of OgilvyOne. Some occurred outside the company, in social gatherings and on their own personal time. They conversed during sports events, in bars and restaurants, and on weekend retreats. We know that these low-key social events are crucial to the development of generalized trust and to the connectivity of a Hot Spot. They establish what has been termed the "third space," a neutral ground. It is in this third space that rank is forgotten and conversation is the center of the entertainment. It is here that playful exchanges can take place.[18]

Polly and Carlos at BP are also members of a company that places a premium on purposeful conversation. The management team at BP explicitly focuses on enhancing the depth, breadth, and quality of conversations at all levels in the organization as a means to supporting learning. As Deputy CEO Rodney Chase described it, "One of the most pressing reasons to create a dialogue . . . has been the rise of connectivity within the space in which BP operates. There are people who by dint of communications, flexibility, and immediacy have the capacity to find things out and transmit the information instantaneously."

Bonding conversations are crucial to the evolution of the connectivity of a Hot Spot. Over time, these bonding conversations are balanced with the need to develop a means by which heedful interaction can take place.

Heedful interaction

Let us return for a moment to Tim and Nigel as they work to merge their companies. As they get to know each other better and begin to trust each other, the nature of their conversation changes. Over time, more of their conversations will be engaged with dealing with the known and established day-to-day operations of their merged company. In this heedful interaction, they will be taking close note of what the other says and will be acting on it and giving feedback and comments. Although these conversations about established knowledge may on the face of it seem routine, this is rarely the case. In fact, for Tim and Nigel and their team, these repeated patterns of behavior are important in establishing their own and their team's shared understanding. It is during these heedful conversations that the tacit knowledge each has about their firm, its products, and its clients is understood and exchanged.

Heedful interactions can be face to face. They can also be virtual. Take, for example, the virtual communications that are a crucial aspect of the Hot Spots that emerge across Linux. When Amit and his Linux colleagues are working on a problem, attention, conscientiousness, and vigilance are high. For others like Polly and Carlos at BP, much of their telephone conversations and meetings will consist of heedful interaction. The problem they are solving provides time and encouragement for "conversing while doing." These heedful interactions are crucial to the life and ultimately to the productivity of a Hot Spot.

Not all relationships in a Hot Spot need to be high-trust, but the more of those there are, the more they create a general feeling about trust and goodwill that influences the relationships around them. These high-trust relationships are also likely to develop and remain robust when they are "multidimensional"—that is, these relationships are not built on one way of relating and transacting with each other but rather on many ways of relating to each other. Ultimately, these multidimensional relationships are more intimate than single-stranded relationships. Their strength and complexity ensure that they are more likely to remain strong, even under pressure.

Crossing Boundaries Through Boundary Spanners

People who have experience in spanning boundaries and are willing and able to introduce people across their networks can have a profoundly positive impact on the emergence and health of Hot Spots. They are one aspect of the glue of connectivity that holds a Hot Spot together. This raises a number of questions: Is everyone a potential boundary spanner? What value do boundary spanners create in a Hot Spot? Can a Hot Spot have too many boundary spanners?

The personality of the boundary spanner

The preference of some boundary spanners to connect people they know and to work across boundaries reflects a stable personality trait known as self-monitoring.[19] High self-monitors are in a sense hard-wired to bridge boundaries. They do so by being adept at changing their way of behaving as they move from one group to another. This change can involve a change in cognitions and even in language. These high self-monitors are able to move from one group to another and become particularly skilled at picking up and responding to the subtle norms of behavior in each group. They are chameleons who tend to be especially sensitive and skilled in bridging interests, professions, and organizations. High self-monitors are adept at acquiring an understanding of people and organizations outside their own circles and therefore have the capacity to acquire and value differences in others with regard to culture or mindset. Low self-monitors prefer to act in the same way regardless of the situation they are in. As a consequence, their preference is not to bridge boundaries, for to do so would force them to modify their behavior to suit the group they are in.

Our basic personality traits may play a role in whether we adopt boundary-spanning behavior. We can also gain boundary-spanning ability as a result of our past experience of working across boundaries. This past experience of spanning boundaries can be crucial to the development of the networks of a Hot Spot as a result of its heritage of ties. As boundary spanners move across boundaries, they take with them a whole host of relationships (some strong ties, some weak ties, and some latent ties) they have forged in the past. These relationships, when introduced into a new network, can bring fresh new ideas, frameworks, and metaphors. This is particularly the case for boundary-spanning experience that crosses company sectors and geographies. These boundary spanners are more likely to bring with them ideas and insights that are more novel than those who have simply jumped functions or moved to same-sector companies. The insights and views of adept boundary spanners may result in the questioning of basic paradigms and ways of working. These can result in major shifts or discontinuous innovations.[20]

It is an interesting notion to think about who gains from the skills of boundary spanners. In some cases, they are bridging between groups where there is little or no overlap between the knowledge currently held by the members of the two groups. Instead there exists between the two groups what has been termed a "structural hole" with regard to knowledge.[21]

Who gets the value created by boundary spanners? There is a strong argument, particularly from behavioral economists, that boundary spanners who bridge structural holes have a wonderful opportunity to *arbitrage*. They do this by bringing the knowledge and ideas from one group to another group that does not yet possess this knowledge.

Boundary spanners are valuable to a Hot Spot because they have the the capacity and motivation to bridge in a manner that widens rather than narrows the networks. The crucial capacity here is the boundary spanner's preparedness and ability to introduce people in his or her cross-boundary networks to each other. To create value in a Hot Spot, a boundary spanner must actively introduce people to each other who might have a common work interest and whom the spanner believes might benefit from knowing each other. People skilled in this will describe issues in a way that will appeal to a diverse set of interests. They will also see opportunities for members of their network to collaborate with each other and will forge links between people dealing with similar issues. This motivation to connect others is partly a personality trait, partly past experience, and partly learned from the executives, practices, and processes of the company.

Too much emphasis on boundary spanners and boundary-spanning activities can decrease the coherence of the team and result in fragmentation of activities.[22] The value of boundary spanners depends on the particular phase of the Hot Spot. At the early stages of a Hot Spot, they are crucial to understanding the context in which the task is being formulated. Their exposure to other groups and networks, such as the market, customers and competitors, can be useful to the mission of the group as it is described and understood. However, as the group gets down to the task at hand, too much boundary spanning can distract. What the group needs is to get on with making ideas work rather than being bombarded with other ideas. So for boundary spanners to be successful throughout the life of a Hot Spot, there will be times when it is appropriate for them to stifle their natural tendencies.

◉ The Role of Executives in Supporting and Enabling Boundary Spanning

When people in Hot Spots actively work across boundaries, they have the potential to create value through new combinations. To do this, they have to face the challenges of being distant, being different, and working with strangers. They can meet these challenges by developing the habit of purposeful conversation and by actively valuing and using the capabilities of boundary spanners.

What role, if any, can executives play in shaping a context in which cross-boundary working is more likely to emerge? Where Hot Spots flourish, executives support cross-boundary working in three key ways. First, they invest in social activities that encourage people from across the company to meet; next, they make use of technology to support cross-boundary working; and finally, they use a portfolio of practices and processes to encourage the formation of network ties across boundaries.

Investing in cross-company social activities

Recall that multidimensional relationships, where people know something of others beyond their work life, are potentially stronger relationships than those that are single-stranded. Multidimensional relationships flourish where there are social activities during which people can relax and get to know each other. In my own research, my colleagues and I measured the extent and frequency of social activities. We found that companies and groups where trust and reciprocity were high had made a more significant investment in social activities. These social activities give people a chance to get to know each other outside the context of work and to learn about each other in a more relaxed way.

Social activities are helpful because over time, companies with a dense network of strong, multidimensional relationships develop a context of generalized trust that encourages Hot Spots to emerge and flourish. This context of trust strengthens as time goes on, and with it comes strong expectations of trust and abstention from opportunism.[23] Highly opportunistic, self-interested behavior becomes increasingly delegitimized and cooperative, trusting behavior legitimized. This network of trusting relationships can be enormously valuable both to the company and to individuals. Recall the transaction costs of Toyota and General Motors. As Toyota found, the greater the reliance on trust, the less the risks inherent in a transaction, and as a consequence, the less the company needed to invest in costly monitoring and control procedures

Widening the net of involvement

Companies with more than their fair share of Hot Spots are adept at supporting the development of strong, lasting relationship ties. They are also adept at enabling networks of weak ties to emerge across the boundaries of the company. As you saw in Figure 4.3, these networks of weak ties ensure that innovative and thought-provoking ideas can emerge between people who are very different. By actively shaping and widening the net of involvement, executives in these companies are avoiding our natural tendency to create networks with people similar to ourselves.

This takes insight and thought. Think for a moment about your own company and the way that groups such as project teams and task forces are assembled. My bet is that in many situations, these project teams and task forces are constructed with the same people. Simply put, the net has been cast in the immediate vicinity.

If productive, creative, and innovative Hot Spots are to emerge, executives have to widen the net of involvement. They do this by inviting enthusiasts from across the company, by pulling on the weak ties in the organization rather than simply relying on the strong ties, and by encouraging a spirit of volunteerism. (We will return to this concept of volunteerism in Chapter 5 when we take a closer look at the telecom company BT.)

Using technology to widen the net of involvement

Executives skilled in creating context in which Hot Spots can emerge realize that for enthusiasts to join a Hot Spot, they need to know about it and need to have heard the igniting question. So these executives go to great lengths to communicate the igniting questions within nascent Hot Spots, sometimes using rather sophisticated technology to assist them.

The executives at OgilvyOne are masters at doing just that. When Tim and his team joined OgilvyOne, they quickly became accustomed to Truffles. Truffles, you will recall, is an integrated community technology system designed to harness the brainpower of the corporation, including marketing gurus, mathematicians, statisticians, strategy consultants, and the individuals on the creative staff.

Truffles provides not only a database and system for testing ideas and hypotheses but also opportunities for people to generate new ideas together through various chat rooms, bulletin boards, and dedicated forums. For example, within weeks of joining OgilvyOne, a number of Tim's colleagues from NoHo had joined the Truffles chat rooms to talk about the likely implications of 3G (third generation mobile technology). Within days, they were up to speed with the ideas around 3G and had added their own thoughts and assumptions. That meant that when Nigel, Tim, and his colleagues became excited about an igniting question around the future of 3G, they were able to rapidly communicate their initial ideas to a wide community of people who were then able to contribute to the conversations in the chat rooms. By creating platforms of communication technology, executives at OgilvyOne had provided a means through which people could volunteer to join nascent Hot Spots.

The infrastructure that supports the creation of networks of strong and weak ties is typically rather comprehensive. Recall from Chapter 2 how the ties between Polly and Carlo at BP were supported and encouraged by BP's signature process: peer groups and peer assist. These practices together forged an environment of trust and reciprocity that encouraged the emergence of the productive Hot Spot that formed between Poland and Venezuela.

To get a better feel for the comprehensive infrastructure that supports the creation of strong and weak ties, let us take a closer look at how executives in Nokia developed a portfolio of practices and processes that widen the net of involvement. We will also take a closer look at Nokia's signature process, modular architecture.

How Nokia Widens the Net of Involvement

Nokia devotes much effort to widening the net of involvement through the use of every day practices and processes.[24] You can understand this comprehensive infrastructure by returning to Figure 4.3, in connection with which we considered the impact the depth of relationships and the extent of boundary spanning had on knowledge sharing and exploring. Let us now take the same figure and plot onto it the various practices and processes employed at Nokia to influence the formation of ties and ultimately the extent and type of knowledge creation.

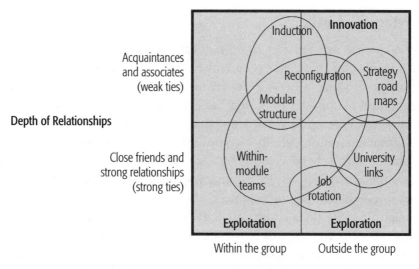

Figure 4.6 The five practices and processes at Nokia that influence the formation of relationships

Five key practices and processes (strategy road maps, induction, university links, job rotation, and the modular structure that has elements of both within-module teams and reconfiguration across teams) are positioned on the matrix in Figure 4.6. Some, such as the "strategy road map" process, have the effect of creating weak ties that span boundaries outside the group. Recall from our discussion of Figure 4.3 that it is in these networks of weak cross-boundary ties that value can be created through innovation. Other practices are more likely to create the strong ties that bridge group boundaries. It is in these networks of strong cross-boundary ties that value occurs through exploration. There are also practices that develop and retain strong ties within a group. These are crucial to the understanding and exploitation of tacit knowledge. At Nokia, those modular teams who stay together over time are a key element of Nokia's signature modular structure. As you will see, the capacity of the executive team of a company to develop a sufficiently wide portfolio of practices and processes is crucial to its capacity to encourage the emergence of Hot Spots. Let us take a closer look at these five practices.

Strategy road maps

Strategy road maps play an important role in the emergence of weak ties that form across the business and functional boundaries of Nokia. In the strategy road map process, every six months, the members of the senior team meet to consider what they believe will be the five or six key challenges over the coming years. These challenges, which often take the form of igniting questions, are then communicated to employees throughout Nokia. Within a short period of time, people and groups coalesce around these igniting questions. The sponsoring executives appoint some group members, while others are volunteers. As a consequence, within a week of the igniting questions being posed, hundreds of people from across the businesses and functions of Nokia are working on them together. For the next month, members of these Hot Spots work under intense pressure to understand their chosen igniting question and to identify their options.

This process of strategic project teams has been crucial to the innovative performance of Nokia. In the view of the executive team members, the practice of bringing people together from across the company has underpinned a series of innovations the company was able to bring to the marketplace. According to Nokia's CEO, "It certainly improved the quality of our bets." For example, the initial thinking about the development of the N-gage mobile phone and video game, at a total investment of over $600 million, was started in one of these sessions. So was the decision to significantly change the new product pipeline by fast-tracking some products in anticipation of Motorola's changing from the Symbian operating system to that offered by Microsoft.

By bringing relative strangers together, ignited by a fascinating question, the executive team at Nokia has created an environment in which Hot Spots naturally emerge. This continual making and breaking of network relationships achieves just the right level of innovation and new combinations.

University links

There are companies and industry sectors where "blue-sky research" would be of little interest, but this is not the case in the dynamic and technically sophisticated competitive environment in which Nokia operates. Although much effort goes into creating technology teams within the company, much effort is also expended linking these teams to their technological counterparts in universities. As a consequence, there are strong and intensive relationship ties between members of Nokia and the faculty of about twenty institutions of higher learning around the world who are working in areas of direct interest to the Nokia executives. There are also less frequent and less intense ties between members of Nokia and about one hundred other universities.

Job rotation

The creation of strong ties that cross boundaries is particularly influenced by the attitude of the senior team to career experiences. Nokia executive team members have typically changed their roles every couple of years. Below the executive team are a group of two hundred to three hundred key people; they too rotate through jobs every three to five years. To facilitate this breadth of job experience, most job vacancies are advertised on the Nokia internal portal, and people are encouraged to apply for jobs outside their immediate role.

As people jump into new businesses, countries, functions, and teams, they initially establish weak ties. Over time, some of these relationships will strengthen and become strong ties. As people subsequently move, they will take with them some of their old strong ties and introduce them to members of their current group.

The philosophy at Nokia around job change is that after three to five years, most people are operating in their comfort zone, and it is time for them to do something completely different. For example, one senior executive, Korhonen, went from R&D to operations to logistics and then to mobile software. These job leaps typically take place across countries, across functions, or across processes. Occasionally they involve jumping all three boundaries at one time. Korhonen reports, "I have continuously been thrown into cold water and have had to learn to swim. I have done jobs for which I have had no experience. It is the spirit of entrepreneurship and trust. For example, at the age of thirty-one, I was given the job to run the European factories and manufacturing technology globally. At that time, I had only been to a factory a couple of times. It is all about degrees of trust." This preference for the spirit of entrepreneurship and trust is also apparent in the induction practices of Nokia.

Induction

When a newcomer joins Nokia or takes a new role, a well-established induction practice takes place. The induction practice is strikingly simple but also strikingly effective. In the first few weeks of joining, the newcomer will be formally introduced by his or her manager to six people from within the team and to six people outside the team. This has two important effects that favor the emergence of a Hot Spot. First, it kick-starts the strong ties within groups that may be crucial to the Hot Spot, and second, it begins development of the weak ties across boundaries that are crucial to the development of generalized trust. The practice also legitimizes and encourages people to cross boundaries and supports the role of the boundary spanner. As a consequence, even within weeks of joining Nokia or taking a new role, people are developing relationships with people very different from themselves.

Modular structure

One of the striking aspects of Nokia is its signature modular structure. As Mikko Kosonen, senior vice president of strategy and business information, points out, "One of the distinctive characteristics of Nokia is the organizational architecture. It is avant-garde. It fits with the turbulence and an opportunity-rich environment [and it has] reconfigurable, modular, reusable capabilities."

Nokia's structural architecture is unique. It is a signature process that has been developed over a long period of time and is vigorously supported by senior executives.

A glance at Figure 4.6 shows that the real skill of the modular architecture is that it creates islands of continuity and stability (through strong ties within groups) while at the same time creating flux and change (through weak ties across groups). Nokia's architecture typically involves new combinations of existing module teams. This sleight of hand enables these intact teams with strong trusting relationships to remain together and retain and refine their tacit knowledge over extended periods of time, even as the structural architecture around them changes. However, these intact modular teams are unlikely to be places where new novel combinations arise. This innovation capacity is more likely to be located in the many weak ties that bridge the boundaries of the company and are created by the reconfiguration of intact module teams.

The structural modularity of Nokia's architecture is built up from a common platform that delivers a single system (termed "value domains") for logistics, human resources, finances, and other transactions. Sitting on this common platform are a number of business groups and core horizontal processes. The common platform and value domains at Nokia create a base on which frequent and rapid reconfigurations can take place. At any moment, reconfigurations can involve changes in the business groups and/or changes in the value domains.

This structural architecture is unique to Nokia and reflects the heritage and values of the firm. Nokia has been a leader in software technology since the 1980s. Like the company's software technology, its modular structure is built from two core elements: the software concept of reusability and standardization through the creation of a shared common platform. In the same way that modular reconfiguration ensures that valuable software is not lost, the same philosophy ensures that valuable skills, competencies, and team relationships among modular teams of people are not lost or diluted. In software programs, the modular units that are reconfigured are pieces of written software. In the company architecture, the modular units that are reconfigured are modular teams of people with similar competencies and skills.

The discipline, philosophy, and mindset of reconfiguration through standardization and shared platforms, initially developed from its technology history, has ensured that Nokia is able to skillfully and rapidly reconfigure its human resources to meet changing customer needs.

The signature process of modularity at Nokia is also, in its essence, an embodiment of the company's values. At Nokia, executives say that Finnish cultural values have played a key role in shaping the environment of the company. The culture of Finland has historically sprung from the values of trust, directness, and inclusively in social relationships. Like other Scandinavians, the Finns have an abhorrence of hierarchical authority and a fundamental belief in respect for the individual.[25] At the same time, Finland has been a country of renewal. It has one of the highest education rates in the world and one of the most technically literate populations. As a nation, Finland has renewed itself, and as a company, Nokia has attempted to do the same. Over the history of Nokia, these Finnish values of respect for the individual and renewal became deeply embedded in a company that was, in its executive team, essentially Finnish. These values of renewal and respect permeate the company's modular structure. This structure embodies a respect for individuals by enabling people to work primarily in collegial teams to which they bring their own competencies. At the same time, the capacity of the structure to be rapidly reconfigured ensures that renewal can take place.

As you have seen, there is much executives and employees can do to shape a mindset of cooperation and develop practices and processes to encourage and value boundary spanning. Both these elements are crucial to the stimulating the latent energy of Hot Spots. However, they are not sufficient. For the energy of a Hot Spot to be ignited, people need a purpose. It is to this third element of a Hot Spot, the igniting purpose, that we now turn.

CHAPTER SUMMARY

THE SECOND ELEMENT: BOUNDARY SPANNING

Key Points

- Extensive use of cross-functional task forces and project teams

- Induction practices in which newcomers are formally introduced to people inside and outside their immediate team

- Informal socialization practices that encourage informal connections across boundaries

- Practices and processes that encourage cross-boundary participation

- Selection, development, and training of boundary spanners

- Succession-planning practices that encourage lateral job moves

New Rules

- **Value creation.** Value in companies is created by exploiting what is already known through strong relationship ties. Novelty and innovation emerge through exploration; this is facilitated by networks of relationships that cross boundaries. Be absolutely aware which type of value creation is appropriate, and influence the emergence of networks around this.

- **Boundary spanners.** Hot Spots become moribund without boundary spanners. Boundary spanners bring insights from others that result in more diffuse networks and potential paradigm shifts. However, be aware that the role is complex and can at times be distracting. Be committed to boundary spanners; nurture and cherish them.

5

THE THIRD ELEMENT: IGNITING PURPOSE

> Hot Spots = (Cooperative Mindset x Boundary Spanning x _Igniting Purpose_) x Productive Capacity

A COOPERATIVE MINDSET sets the stage for performance. Boundary spanning increases the probability of innovation through exploration. Both of these elements are fundamentally stage setters. They lay the foundations for Hot Spots, but they do not by themselves spark Hot Spots. In a productive Hot Spot, there has to be a point of ignition. It is at this point that all the latent energy contained within the cooperative mindset and the cross-boundary working is released. It is at this point that the thermal goggles lens referred to earlier reveals a bright red Hot Spot in the midst of green and blue. Recall from Figure 1.3, reproduced here as Figure 5.1, that the igniting purpose generally takes one of three forms.

- **An igniting vision.** Some Hot Spots are ignited through a compelling vision of the future. This is often created by the leaders of the company or else by highly creative and often

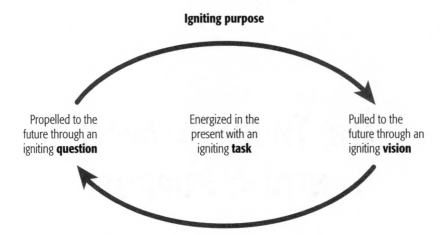

Igniting purpose

Propelled to the
future through an
igniting **question**

Energized in the
present with an
igniting **task**

Pulled to the
future through an
igniting **vision**

Figure 5.1 Forms an igniting purpose can take

maverick individual contributors. This vision in a sense pulls the latent energy of a cooperative mindset and boundary spanning into the future. As a consequence, when people become part of a Hot Spot, the coordinating mechanism that helps them cooperate is their shared vision of what can be achieved.

- **An igniting question.** An igniting vision pulls latent energy into a Hot Spot with the catalyst of a shared vision of the future. Yet many Hot Spots don't have this all-encompassing vision of the future. In these Hot Spots, the latent energy is released by being propelled into the future. The propelling force is an igniting question that is capable of creating sufficient curiosity and enthusiasm to release the latent energy. The people in the Hot Spot may not know where their journey will take them, but they collectively understand the question they are trying to answer.

- **An igniting task.** Both the igniting vision and the igniting question are essentially about the future. But the third type of ignition is firmly based in the reality of the present. This is the igniting task. In Hot Spots ignited by a task, what really excites and motivates people is the opportunity to work on something that is intriguing, ambiguous, and potentially highly developmental.

Although I have described these three ignition points as separate, in reality, Hot Spots can be ignited by a combination. Take the ignition for

Linux as an example. The ignition here was a vision about open-source platforms; this was quickly followed by a way of working and a task that was intriguing and exciting.

Pulled to the Future Through an Igniting Vision

When Amit joined the Linux community, he became a member of a Hot Spot ignited by the vision of Richard Stallman and Linus Torvalds. The vision that Stallman had was of a world of open-source programs. He believed that these programs could be developed in the same way that academics develop theory, with groups of people with open access to each other's work building on each other's research. This was the vision that ignited the Hot Spot that became Linux. Carolyn Kenwood describes Stallman's vision: "In the proprietary model, individuals or small groups of individuals quietly and reverently develop software in isolation, without releasing a beta version before it is deemed ready. In contrast, the open source model relies on a network of 'volunteer' programmers, with different styles and agendas, who develop and debug the code in parallel."[1]

Here is a vision and also the possibility of a way of working that is enticing and exciting. It was this igniting vision that people across the world responded to. In my own research, my colleagues and I found a similar genesis in many Hot Spots: they were ignited by the vision of an individual or a small group and then developed by a wider group of people.

Take Wikipedia, for example. Here is how Wikipedia's cofounder, Jimmy Wales, set the vision: "Imagine a world in which every single person is given free access to the sum of all human knowledge. That's what we're doing. And we need your help. Our vision is to create and distribute a multilingual free encyclopedia of the highest possible quality to single people on the planet in their own language."[2]

The energy latent in many people was ignited by this vision, and the Wikipedia community was born. In 2003, the database contained less than one gigabyte; by 2004, it had two gigabytes; by 2005, it had five gigabytes; and was over eight by the end of 2006. With more than a million articles, it has content in English, German, Japanese, Spanish, Dutch, Polish, Italian, and French. It has attracted over one hundred thousand volunteer contributors from all over the world, and it gets more visitors than the online *New York Times,* CNN, and other mainstream sites.

Wikipedia is fundamentally based on peer-to-peer conversation. Wikis are Web pages that allow anybody to log in and make changes. These communities require trust, so how do over one hundred thousand people trust each other? In fact, fewer than 1 percent of all visitors make most of the edits. These add up to a few hundred committed volunteers. As Jimmy Wales comments, "This becomes a real community of people who know each other and value their reputations."

Propelled to the Future Through an Igniting Question

There are occasions during Hot Spots when an inspirational character has a vision that is sufficiently compelling to ignite latent energy. However, being pulled to the future by a vision is not the only way Hot Spots are ignited. Often the point of ignition is not a vision of what the future could be but rather a question. What ignites the latent energy is the spark of a question that is so intriguing that it is capable of unleashing latent energy. These igniting questions typically have sufficient depth to generate emotional passion and intellectual sparkle. The mundane, the obvious, the inevitable just does not do it.

The way that Polly and Carlos at BP cooperated across boundaries was partly a result of BP's signature peer assist and peer challenge processes. What also stoked Polly, Carlos, and many of their colleagues was the igniting question of how the company could serve as a "force for good." The igniting question CEO John Browne and his colleagues actually asked was this: "How can a large oil company create value in the world rather than simply be an exploiter of natural resources?" From this igniting question came many initiatives. One such initiative was the emergence of a team of interested people who called themselves the "Ignite Group." Conversations throughout BP led many people to make commitments to becoming a force for good. These commitments included significant investments in alternative energy sources and a reevaluation of the company's policy in many parts of the developing world.

Energized in the Present with an Igniting Task

The latent energy in Hot Spots is also ignited by the nature of the work itself. One of the threads that runs through early stories of Hot Spots is the delight people take in the task in which they are engaged. An igniting vision can be very compelling, and the "big question" can make a real difference. Beyond these points of ignition is the idea that latent energy is released through exciting work. Take, for example, the way in which the senior team at BT ignited the latent energy of the company through a simple process called the Challenge Cup.

The Challenge Cup at BT

Like most telecom companies, BT has gone through some tough times. In 1990, the company employed just under 250,000 people; by 2006, it was down to 100,000—not, you might imagine, a promising place for Hot Spots to emerge. Yet our research showed that BT has more than its fair share of Hot Spots. An example of the ignition of the latent energy within BT was the challenge of a task that excited and energized people from across the company.

In 2004, Pierre Danon, CEO of BT's Retail Division, set a challenge to the company to make a real positive difference in customers' experiences of BT. The quest was to crown one team the Supreme Champions of Customer Satisfaction. The rules of the game were simple. Anyone could participate—all that employees had to do was form a team of eight like-minded people and then recruit a team coach and a sponsor to support them through the competition. Any idea was permissible; it simply had to be focused on increasing customers' satisfaction. The third rule was perhaps the most interesting. Joining a team was not mandatory; employees did not have to join, nor was it part of their job description or performance review. People simply volunteered, choosing to give their time . . . or not.

The initial challenge kicked off in 2004 with 450 teams choosing to take part. The second tournament ran in 2005, with participants from the first tournament as powerful advocates and coaches. Each team worked up their ideas and insights over a period of months, and of the 540 entries, 300 teams made it through to the quarterfinals and were given the resources to work up their ideas.

The prize? The joy of working in Hot Spots—and the pleasure of the Challenge Cup. The outcome? For individuals, the wonderful feeling of recognition and appreciation, of working on a task that was challenging, meaningful, and exciting. Plus the chance to meet and work with new people, to hone new skills and develop new talents. For BT, the outcome was productivity improvements that at last count amounted to £42 million and a marked increase in engagement, enthusiasm, and customer focus.

These igniting tasks, like BT's Challenge Cup, typically have a number of characteristics in common. First, people engaged in a Hot Spot believe that what they are doing is meaningful both to them and to others. The task itself is challenging, exciting, and ambiguous. And the task provides an opportunity for personal and group development and learning.

Ambiguous challenge

This was one of the really interesting insights from our cooperative research study. One of the survey questions was the extent to which the task participants engaged in was ambiguous and complex. Our working assumption was that ambiguous tasks would be more difficult, and therefore boundary-less cooperation would be more unlikely. To our surprise, the results of the study did not support this assumption. On the contrary, when we talked further to people about this, we found that ambiguous tasks are more interesting, more complex, and more igniting of latent cooperation.

Significance and meaning

The meaningfulness of a task plays a key role in igniting latent energy. Meaningful tasks resonate with one's sense of values. The people working on Wikipedia, for example, continue to donate their energy and talent because the task resonates with their own values that knowledge should be free to all and with the pleasure they get from mastery of their chosen area of knowledge. Our tasks are also meaningful when we believe they have an impact on others or on the company. We are more likely to cooperate and engage when we believe that what we do can make a difference—that it has an impact. People working on the "force for good" initiative at BP or for Linux believe that however small the extent, their contributions and energy create something that has impact and meaning.

Opportunity for development

The task's developmental capacity can ignite latent energy. This developmental capability can be focused on any or all of the three aspects of human capital. We are more likely to be engaged with and enthused by a task that provides an opportunity to develop our knowledge and know-how. It could be a task that develops our social capital with opportunities for us to span boundaries and to enhance our network, or it could be a task in which we have an opportunity to develop our emotional capital through increased self-awareness or feedback. The actual developmental focus is unique to each task. Yet no matter how development occurs, it can play a crucial role in ignition.

Energy can be ignited in three important ways—ignition can also fail. Instead of the passion of Hot Spots, the inertia of a the country club sets in.

When Purpose Fails: Emergence of the Country Club

When latent energy fails to ignite, the Big Freeze spreads across the landscape. This can occur if there are no passionate debates about the future; no big, intriguing questions; no complex and ambiguous tasks. When this occurs, instead of the passion of ignition, we see the complacency of what I call the country club. The country club is a place where people are comfy, subdued, and predictable. It contains none of the fire and excitement of a Hot Spot.

Why does ignition fail? One of the most striking causes is an absence of purposeful conversation. Recall that purposeful conversations—containing both bonding conversations and heedful interactions—play a crucial role in supporting the creation of relationships that span boundaries. Conversations also play a role as a catalyst in igniting purpose. The conversations in country clubs are often mundane and obvious, ritualized talk that is neither stimulating nor relevant. People in country club situations often find themselves caught in an unfocused, distracted working life. Rather than big igniting questions, people converse around the known, the trite, the safe, and the boring. Conversation becomes what the philosopher David Whyte refers to as "dehydrated talk."[3]

Sometimes these dehydrated conversations are set pieces, as at the strategy meeting where everyone knows what to say and how to respond, where nothing new is discovered, nothing unusual is aired—just the mundane camouflaged as the exciting. On these occasions, no visions are described, no big questions are asked, no intriguing tasks are designed. Too often this occurs because we are victims of tightly defined agendas that constrain the opportunities for exploration or discovery, victims of schedules that are so tight that there is little opportunity for pause or reflection or for the flow of insight and thoughtfulness. Dehydrated talk can emerge as a result of constraints built into the physical space—the one-to-one across a boss's desk or around a rectangular table. Or dehydrated talk can become a proxy for downward, hierarchical communication where both parties maintain the pretence that this is an open discussion rather than instruction or even subjugation.

Good Conversation

When Hot Spots emerge, they do so as a product of conversation.[4] They emerged from the conversations about a "force for good" that coursed around BP for a couple of years. They emerged from the conversations at Nokia that turned a potential disaster in China into a triumph. They emerged from the conversations at Wikipedia, where hundreds of people converse virtually about content. As David Weinberger, a fellow at Harvard University's Berkham Center, has reflected, in the field of mainstream media, communities like Wikipedia are rapidly reinventing the rules of the game as conversations: "'Mainstream media,' he remarks, 'don't get how subversive it is to take institutions and turn them into conversations.' That is because institutions are closed, assume a hierarchy, and have trouble admitting fallibility, whereas conversations are open-ended, assume equality, and eagerly concede fallibility."[5]

It is energetic conversations that "eagerly concede fallibility" that spark latent energy. These conversations rarely go from boss to subordinate; they are more likely to be peer-to-peer, colleague-to-colleague, friend-to-friend. Conversations that ignite a Hot Spot are rarely about simply sharing knowledge. They are more often about novel associations, connections, or hunches. The Oxford-based philosopher Theodore Zeldin is passionate about conversation. In his description of conversation, we can sense some of the excitement and energy of Hot Spots. "Conversation," he writes, "is a meeting of minds with different memories and habits. When minds meet, they don't just exchange facts: they transform them, reshape them, draw different implications from them, engage in new trains of thought. Conversation doesn't just reshuffle the cards: it creates new cards."[6]

Igniting questions and the conversations that follow come in a variety of forms. Some are positive and exuberant; others, dark and brooding. They often begin between two people and rarely involve more than four.[7] What is discussed is spontaneous, open-ended, and tentative. The following description captures it delightfully: "immediate in its claim on attention, instantaneous in its moment-to-moment occurrence, and fleeting or ephemeral in its form."[8] For the psychologist Karl Weick, big questions and the good conversations that follow them are much like the jazz he loves to hear: collective improvising, with people listening to others and listening to themselves, using mutual elaboration and spontaneous invention, all within an underlying structure.[9] For Weick, conversation is collaborative and coevolving.

Conversation is the source of the revitalization that sparks the purpose that ignites Hot Spots. These revitalizing sparks of conversation have brought energy and insight throughout the history of civilization. The rise of Romanticism in eighteenth-century Europe revitalized the then moribund continent and paved the way for a dazzling burst of creativity in literature, the arts, the sciences, and philosophy. From Rousseau to Byron, Romantics asked big, broad questions. They set off a whole network of conversations in salons and coffee shops in Vienna and Berlin, Paris and Amsterdam. People met to talk about the purpose of art in society, the impact of industrialization, the aspects and impacts of the natural world. Many of the most profound contributions of that period came out of those conversations.

In companies, we tend to shy away from the big questions. I guess this should come as no surprise. In the field of management, pragmatism has served as the dominant paradigm. As pragmatists, we have focused on the day-to-day reality of living, eschewing the big, broad, "meaning of life" questions as irrelevant. As work became more specialized, more fragmented, and more routinized, our conversations became more pragmatic. Welcome to the country club! We delegitimized the deep, overarching questions, preferring to deal with specifics and immediacies and assuming that taking care of the parts would take care of the whole.

Yet when these big questions are asked, Hot Spots are often ignited. The viselike grip of relentless pragmatism is softened by the invigorating spirit of Romanticism. How can we re-create the spontaneity and excitement of good conversation, conversations packed with rational data and facts and tempered with values and beliefs?

Rational data and facts

The big igniting questions often have elements of both the rational and the emotional, and in fact it is this combination of the two that is crucial. Many of the best conversations have a strong element of rational data and facts triggering challenging inquiries. Imagine the philosopher Socrates in 450 B.C. strolling across the avenues of ancient Athens. His delight was to cross-examine his fellow citizens about the important issues of the day. Socrates used conversation as a way of enabling and engaging people in a systematic and logical examination of facts, assumptions, and beliefs and encouraged his fellow citizens to do the same. Indeed, his approach is known even to this day as the Socratic method.

Many igniting questions have the same logical and rational roots. Take the question that Pertti and his colleagues faced. It was the rational and logical data about Nokia's market position in Asia that unleashed a host of conversations from Asia to Scandinavia. This rational examination of the facts was also an important igniter of the Hot Spots at BP. Deputy CEO Rodney Chase put it this way: "We are a deeply questioning team. We constantly inspect what we do in order to find out if in fact it is the exercise of laziness or prejudice." This focus on rigor and disciplined debate is an important part of the way BP's highly cerebral CEO, John Browne, conducts his conversations: "Unless you can lay out rational arguments as the foundations of what you do, nothing much happens" is his constant refrain.

Values and beliefs

Not all igniting questions are drawn strictly from data and rational conversation. Also crucial are a very strong set of values or beliefs. Some of the most energetic Hot Spots are ignited through a combined emotional and rational conversation, fused in a dynamic way. Like the yin and yang of Chinese philosophy, the most creative and insightful, most energizing and igniting conversations in Hot Spots occur when the two occur together: one hard, the other soft; one rooted in the categories of structure, the other in the images of meaning. To bring thinking and feeling together is to move from fragmentation to unity.

This unity of conversation was the ignition for the "force for good" idea at BP—in the words of Rodney Chase, "having goals that are worth pursuing for everyone, that have to do with making society better as a result of our participation than if we had not been there." For twelve months, Hot Spots raged across BP. People from all over the company engaged in purposeful conversations about the fundamental values of the firm and how the values could be expressed into some concrete action, or what came to be called "proof points." The conversations were deeply grounded in facts. With the help of external research partners, the people immersed in the Hot Spots collected an enormous amount of data all the way from industrial trends and government policies to NGO aspirations and employee surveys. Beyond data, the conversations were also about hopes and aspirations from all the people who worked at BP, of various ages, national heritages, and business backgrounds. More than fifteen thousand employees directly participated in these conversations. Their views, expressing a passion that surprised management, shaped the attributes that would underlie the company's new image—progressive, green, innovative, and performance-driven. By the time BP's new slogan, "Beyond Petroleum," was launched, these values and the overall theme of becoming a force for good had created a level of energy, enthusiasm, and commitment among people that was unprecedented in BP's history.

Let's now reflect on what can be done to generate an igniting purpose and ensure that the country club does not invade company territory.

Creating an Igniting Purpose

We cannot will Hot Spots into existence, but we can identify a purpose capable of igniting the latent energy of Hot Spots. The people and companies best able to do this share certain characteristics:

- They engage in constant vigorous yet courteous questioning and inquiry.
- They actively encourage boundary spanning.
- They shape the space and time for refection.

Constant vigorous yet courteous questioning and inquiry

We can ignite the latent energy in our organizations and communities by supporting a culture of constant questioning. Tough questions need to be asked, and tough questions need fuel. Often the fuel from a single work group or business unit is not sufficient. Some of the most interesting igniting questions I have heard came as a result of an individual's or group's exposure to a variety of information and stimuli from inside and outside the company. At Nokia, the links with the faculty of universities around the world brought new insights. At BP, the external stimuli came from the executive team's capacity to build close relationships with faculty from some of the top universities in the world—Cambridge, Stanford, and Yale, for example—and a variety of experts in other institutions.

Sometimes these igniting questions can be difficult. We found that as important in the question itself was legitimizing honest doubt—the capacity to admit one's own doubts and uncertainties. At the heart of Socrates' capacity to question was his own belief that he himself knew nothing. Those who believe they must always have the right answer kill curiosity and inquiry. It takes confidence and courage to acknowledge one's own ignorance.

Encouraging boundary spanning

The igniting question often comes from outside the immediate team. The capacity to cross boundaries can therefore often be crucial to the emergence of the igniting question and indeed to the longer-term creative and innovative health of a Hot Spot. I clearly saw the impact of boundary spanning and a novel combination of insights and knowledge at Tesco, one of the world's largest retailers, with operations in Europe and Asia.

I stumbled across this Hot Spot in conversation with members of the human resource function. Within minutes, they began telling me about a really interesting project they had been engaged in that they believed would add significant value to the work of the function and to the wider Tesco community. I began to sense a Hot Spot. I learned that it had started with one of those classic deceptively simple but igniting questions. One day, the CEO asked Clare Chapman, the head of HR, the following question:

> *Clare, when the head of marketing comes to the executive board meeting, he presents data on our consumers, and we are given enormous insight about their buying habits, their aspirations, their concerns, and their hopes. We have clear demographic data, and we can predict with real accuracy how buying patterns will evolve. But when HR presents information about our employees, it is less precise, less insightful, and less predictive.*
>
> *Clare, why do we know more about our consumers than we know about our employees?*

This is a fascinating igniting question, and it triggered a Hot Spot at Tesco. Within minutes of leaving the board room, Clare talked to the head of marketing's Consumer Insight Unit. She began to realize that the CIU had developed demographic techniques for modeling consumer preferences and intentions that were light-years ahead of anything HR was doing. She talked to her staff, and by the end of the day, a group of people from HR had volunteered to become part of the answer to the question. They had begun to imagine how the CIU techniques could be used for employees rather than consumers. Their initial efforts taught them that the modeling techniques could indeed be adapted. By the end of the week, a Hot Spot was burning bright. Volunteers from marketing and HR had met to explore the challenge. A demonstration of what could be done to profile employees' aspirations had been conducted, and resources were beginning to flow in to support the project.

The CEO's igniting question had been an important detonator for the Hot Spot. His insights came from the fact that he bridged the two communities—he knew what marketing was working on, and he knew the challenges HR faced. It was this novel combination of insights that was to fuel the Hot Spot at Tesco and ultimately lead to the creation of the Employee Insight Unit, which flared for over a year and within two years was being described as one of the most creative HR practices in Europe.[10]

CEOs are not the only boundary spanners who can ask igniting questions. In fact, boundary spanners can be found at all levels in a company, and their presence is vital to the emergence of Hot Spots. These people are able to create networks and bring the outside of the company in.[11]

Shaping the space and time for reflection

The formulation of igniting questions requires courage and connections. It also requires space and time devoted to the activity. Otherwise, the igniting question goes unspoken and unanswered, and the mundane triumphs. For Nigel and his colleagues at OgilvyOne, this had always been understood. For decades, the senior team had met with the company's founder, David Ogilvy, at his personal château in France. More than the beauty of the place, the location personified the larger-than-life figure of David Ogilvy—his passion for creativity, his legendary curiosity, his capacity for friendship and love, his personal generosity—and it generated a very different level of conversations and questions than what would have occurred in the company's board room.

It is often a lack of space and time that overwhelms the igniting question. The layout of the space in which people work can play an important role here. Each Hot Spot has its own idiosyncratic pacing and flow. Flow occurs when periods of intense time pressure are interspersed with periods of calm and reflection. Although speed and pressure are important to getting through relatively straightforward work, the creativity and insights of igniting questions occur when we have space and time to reflect and concentrate.

The psychologist Mihaly Csikszentmihalyi describes this as the state of "flow." It occurs when we are deep in concentration and absorbed in the moment. As he describes, when the depth of direct experience in the unfolding moment is high, attention is withdrawn from the self, and it almost ceases to exist. This state is experienced as "timelessness," a transcendence of both time and self. Time stands still, and in the experience of life, time seems extended.[12]

These times of flow create opportunities for igniting questions, and they also ensure that the creativity of Hot Spots can flourish. The ignition of Hot Spots needs *chronos*—the compression of time, making the most of every moment. Hot Spots also need *kairos*—the extension of time. Between the two, we move from the efficiency of compression to the slack of extending time, from the brainstorming that brings ideas and data to the "brain-stilling" of depth and reflection. Hot Spots emerge from igniting questions that emerge in periods of time-out and solitude that balance social time and time together. Private time is crucial as an opportunity for productive leisure, regeneration, and sense-making.

When all three elements are in place—a mindset of cooperation, boundary spanning, and an igniting purpose—the probability of a Hot Spot emerging is significantly enhanced. This is a wonderful beginning. But it is not enough. For Hot Spots to add significant value to the organization, one more ingredient is essential: productivity. It is to this we turn next.

CHAPTER SUMMARY

The Third Element: Igniting Purpose

Key Points

The latent energy of boundaryless cooperation is ignited by purpose. There are three forms that purpose can take:

- Latent energy can be *propelled* by an igniting question that sparks debate and activity.

- Latent energy can be *pulled* by an igniting vision that creates a future state so vivid that energy and action are directed toward it.

- Latent energy can be *energized* by an igniting task that is meaningful, ambiguous, and developmental.

Without the spark of ignition, the latent energy of the cooperative mindset and boundary spanning work remains latent. The possibility of a Hot Spot emerging recedes, its place taken by a country club atmosphere, devoid of sparkle and excitement.

At the heart of all three forms of igniting purpose are conversations between peers. These conversations give rise to vision, igniting questions, and tasks that are meaningful, ambiguous, and developmental. However, conversation can rapidly become "dehydrated" and ritualistic.

New Rules

- **Ignition and leadership.** The latent energy in boundaryless cooperation is ignited with a spark. It could be the spark of a compelling vision, the novelty of a question, or the excitement of a complex and meaningful task. The responsibility of the leader is to ensure that this spark is created

- **Purposeful conversation.** Conversation is the source of igniting purpose. Support and shape conversation with insightful data, an emphasis on values, and space for reflection.

6

THE FOURTH ELEMENT: PRODUCTIVE CAPACITY

Hot Spots = (Cooperative Mindset x Boundary Spanning x Igniting Purpose) x <u>Productive Capacity</u>

THE HOT SPOT HAS EMERGED. The latent energy of cooperation has been ignited through purpose, and the boundary spanning has created the potential for innovation. But will the Hot Spot be productive? Will this release of latent energy actually create value? The answer depends in part on the productive capacity of the Hot Spot. This capacity can have a very significant effect on Hot Spots, as the formula shows. Productive capacity involves a number of crucial ongoing practices and processes within the Hot Spot. These practices and processes become ever more crucial the more complex the Hot Spot. Recall that the complexity of a Hot Spot can be assessed by the extent of the distance between members, the degree to which the participants differ from each other, and the proportion who are strangers to each other. For value to be created, the more complex the Hot Spot, the greater the emphasis on productive practices.

The more complex a Hot Spot, the greater the need to actively channel the energy into productive outcomes. Complexity is low when members of the Hot Spot are located close to each other, they have many characteristics and experiences in common, and the majority already know each other. Complexity is high when the majority of the members are not in the same place and membership crosses time zones, when the members are different from each other in terms of characteristics and experiences, and when few know each other beforehand.

As Hot Spots become more complex, greater energy must be focused on productive practices. There are five key productive practices, and as shown in Figure 1.4, reproduced here as Figure 6.1, these become ever more important the more complex the Hot Spot. These practices can be a real test of the competence of the people in a Hot Spot. They need a whole range of skills and competencies, many of which are not currently well developed in companies. These productive practices follow a specific sequence, with some important at the start of the Hot Spot and others assuming greater importance as the Hot Spot develops.

Productive Practices

We shall examine the five practices in the sequence in which they often emerge.

Practice 1: appreciating talents. For Hot Spots to be productive, an understanding and appreciation of the specific talents of others must be reached early on.

Practice 2: making commitments. Productive Hot Spots abound with active, public, and explicit commitments between the members.

Practice 3: resolving conflicts. Without the spark of disagreement, Hot Spots can rapidly devolve into country clubs. Unresolved conflict can turn a Hot Spot to ice. Productive Hot Spots harness the potential creative energy of conflict through processes of conflict resolution.

Practice 4: synchronizing time. One of the primary sources of conflict in boundaryless cooperation is conflict over time, particularly when Hot Spots stretch across time zones. Productive Hot Spots use a whole range of techniques to synchronize time.

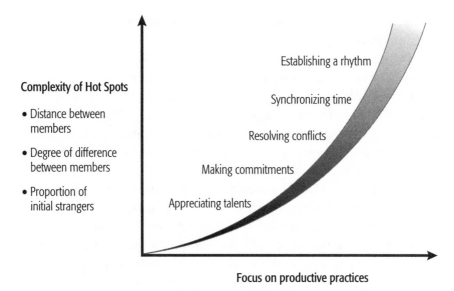

Figure 6.1 Relationship between complexity and productive practices

Practice 5: establishing a rhythm. Hot Spots flounder when the rhythm is wrong: too much pressure, and people burn out; too little pressure, and people lose energy and enthusiasm. Creating a rhythm that works is a crucial task for highly productive Hot Spots.

Typically, in Hot Spots that flourish, at an early phase there was some means by which people understood the talents and skills of others. Of course, this is very simple when they already know each other or of each other's reputation. It is much trickier when they are strangers who knew little of each other beforehand and are not aware of the set of skills and range of knowledge the others have. This appreciation of talents is an important early activity. Without it, nascent Hot Spots rapidly run out of energy as people feel increasingly misunderstood and undervalued.

Some time after this appreciation, members of Hot Spots circle around the igniting question and the goals of their endeavors. Often Hot Spots begin in the blaze of an igniting question or vision. People feel the intellectual sparkle and the emotional passion. Yet inevitably, after this sparkle and passion comes a time of reflection. People began to think more about the question and to converge around it. They begin to understand their role in the Hot Spot and the actions they have to take. For productive Hot Spots, this internal reflection is mirrored with the making of commitments to others.

As people become clearer about what they have to do, the areas of conflict become clearer. This may require a wholesale reanalysis and questioning of the igniting question. There may be challenges about the scope and nature of what has to be achieved and the surfacing of various conflicts inherent in reaching the goal. Simply put, to be productive, members of a Hot Spot must find a way to work together to move from passion, ideas, and innovation to individual and collective action.

Rhythm is crucial to the productive capacity of a Hot Spot. Too much speed and intensity forces people to fall back on old habits, and the creativity of the outcome is lost. Too much speed and intensity also reduces or eliminates time for reflection. Where Hot Spots are productive, the members have found a way to establish a rhythm and also to allow time for reflection.

Practice 1: Appreciating Talents

As a Hot Spot heats up, two important tasks must be accomplished if the Hot Spot is to flourish. There must be some means by which members come to understand the competencies and skills of the other participants, and they must individually and collectively arrive at a clear understanding of what the Hot Spot is about and the igniting purpose.

Participants who fail to understand and appreciate the competencies and skills within the Hot Spot ultimately lose the intellectual sparkle and emotional passion as people begin to feel unappreciated and underutilized. Imagine, for example, if Amit was participating in a developing a code of software at Linux that was far below his level of competence. The excitement and pride he feels, so crucial to his continued volunteer efforts, would be dissipated in his feeling that he was not being stretched. Imagine if Polly contacted Carlos, and Carlos and his team knew nothing about the problems that Polly faced and had no means to develop this knowledge.

Hot Spots ultimately continue to burn because the people in them have the pleasure and pride of contributing something that is important to them. They are understood well enough for their intellectual sparkle to be appreciated and their emotional passion to be heard. Appreciating talents is relatively straightforward when everyone knows one another, has worked with together in the past, and knows the competencies of each participant. When the Hot Spot is complex, made up of people who are neither proximate nor similar, achieving this understanding is much more difficult. Successful Hot Spots inevitably develop some relatively rapid way for everyone in the Hot Spot community to know these things about everyone else. Simply put, the participants quickly come to appreciate each others' talents. Sometimes this is as simple as posting photographs and short biographies in the shared space of the community. In other Hot Spots, people meet face to face at an early stage to socialize and begin to develop the "multidimensional" relationships that can be so important to success.

Knowing what others know is crucial as a Hot Spot heats up because it serves as a platform of information on which some of the issues around participation can be solved. The real issues of participation are who will participate and what they will do. Resolving this is no easy task, for many people in a Hot Spot are working on multiple tasks and projects of which this is only one. So although there are real opportunities for people to be involved, there are also potential costs, conflicts, and dangers. The challenge here is to consider how the various people involved fit into their roles. As the task unfolds, members of a Hot Spot face issues about the allocation of work and the rewards and their expected contribution and payoff.

They also face questions about what they want to achieve and how best to achieve it. In some cases, this is relatively straightforward. There is an ongoing set of challenges, and members of the Hot Spot rapidly coalesce around these issues whenever they arise. For example, the Hot Spots that naturally arise on the assembly lines of Toyota are firmly focused on a specific problem. That's not to say, of course, that there is no need for understanding and negotiation about the nature of the joint activity. But in the main, the problem itself broadly frames the extent and agenda of the Hot Spots.

To a lesser extent, the same is true of Hot Spots that arise around task forces and project teams. In the strategic mapping process at Nokia, for example, or the peer assist process at BP, there was an igniting question that people chose to engage with. For Hot Spots that are less directional and more emergent, issues of clarification are more central. These Hot Spots are fueled by common interest and passion. However, even these more emergent forms of Hot Spots quickly smolder and run out of passion if there is limited agreement of what the Hot Spot is about and what each member could achieve.

I have watched a number of Hot Spots fall apart after what appeared to be a good start. The organizational practices and processes were in place to ensure that people felt positive about Hot Spots, and much had been achieved to create a shared sense of understanding of the skills and talents of individual members and the broad scope of what a particular Hot Spot was about. Yet these Hot Spots fell apart because there was no way in which the inevitable conflicts that arose during this period could be resolved, and people failed to make and then keep their commitments.

Practice 2: Making Commitments

When we work outside a Hot Spot—in a structure of hierarchies and job descriptions—the actions we take are bound by the roles and responsibilities associated with the job we do. The job description makes these roles explicit and clearly states the responsibilities involved. As a consequence, when we perform a task, we simply refer to the role description. This description is often sufficient to ensure that there is agreement about what should be done and who should do it.

Consider for a moment the emergent types of Hot Spots shown in Figure 4.4. When Hot Spots are located within project teams, task forces, or communities of practice, this clarity rarely exists. In fact, as you have seen, much of the invigorating energy of Hot Spots comes precisely because people are involved in complex, ambigious tasks. So if task specification does not shape the relationships within Hot Spots, what does? My own research, as well as that of my colleague at London Business School, Donald Sull, has revealed that the answer is *commitments,* personal promises we make to each other about a future course of action. In the words of Don Sull and Charles Spinosa, commitments are "public, active, voluntary, explicit, and motivated."[1]

Commitment making is particularly important in Hot Spots where much of the conversation and action take place on a peer-to-peer basis. Don Sull would view a Hot Spot as a "nexus of commitments." So just as we can view Hot Spots as networks of relationships, of some strong ties and other weak ties, so too can we view Hot Spots as a dynamic network of interconnected promises that flow from these relationships. These are particularly crucial, as many of the activities in Hot Spots are nonroutine activities for which there is no explicit set of expectations about how the task should be performed.

These commitments can be highly detailed—for example, a clear service agreement between one individual and another. Such a commitment specifies what has been agreed and on what basis satisfaction would be measured. It also specifies the conditions under which the commitment would be binding.

The relationships and performance expectations within BP's peer groups are commitment-based. The philosophy of commitments was built into BP by linking as many conversation processes as possible to tangible and concrete goals. Peer assists, peer reviews, and performance contracts— these are all practices that are primarily aimed at developing intense, purposeful conversations, driven by concrete goals and targets.

Making public commitments

Commitments are most powerful and effective when they are made publicly rather than privately. Hot Spots are essentially supported by the quality and depth of the relationships in them. Although some of these relationships are dyadic, between two people, the majority will be between three or even more. So commitments in Hot Spots are rarely made within dyads. Most are made within the context of triads or more complex relational forms. In essence, these commitments involve many people rather than a few. These public commitments are more binding than private commitments. Since they are made in the context of a network of relationships, there is an element of reputation involved and one of moral obligation. When a commitment is broken, trust is betrayed, and this betrayal is observed by the community.

Making commitments public also has the advantage of broadcasting intentions so that others can comment on potential problems or missed opportunities. At BP, for example, the practice of peer assist makes public the commitment of business unit heads like Polly to support their peers.

Making active commitments

These broad public commitments to support others are followed by detailed, open conversations about the specifics of this assistance. In the case of BP's practice of peer assist, the performance metrics gathered by each business unit head provide a basis for these explicit conversations to take place. It is during this phase of commitment making that those involved hammer out what each has agreed to do. In the words of CEO John Browne:

> *People are challenged the whole time. "Just run that by me one more time" is the mildest challenge. "I don't understand it" to "Surely you've got this wrong" to "No, that is far too conventional and we have to think of a different way," the discussions, debates, and challenges happen everywhere. I participate; everyone participates. If you are sitting*

on the management committee, sometimes it gets very hot indeed. "No, it doesn't make sense"—"Well, make it make sense!" The questions are continuously around.

Making voluntary commitments

Hot Spots are essentially voluntary, emerging forms of activity. People choose to join a Hot Spot and give of their knowledge and insights. They also make a choice to leave a Hot Spot. The network of commitments across a Hot Spot is similarly voluntary. These commitments do not come as part of a role responsibility or job definition; consequently, they are often stronger and more closely aligned to personal responsibility. Each of us knows that we are more likely to meet our commitments when we make them freely rather than under pressure or duress. This notion of volunteering works both ways: in making a commitment and in declining a commitment. Just as Carlos made a voluntary commitment to support Polly's work in Poland, he could have reasonably turned down the request. This is part of the spirit of a Hot Spot, where tasks and activities are not assigned but rather are taken on by people who volunteer to be part of the community of learning.

Making explicit commitments

Commitments are made not by task forces or by committees but by individuals. Commitments start with an individual's taking personal responsibility to engage in an activity. For Amit at Linux, for example, the tasks he performs, the way he engages in them, and the standards he maintains are all commitments he makes. These commitments are more likely to hold when they are explicit enough that individuals know what they must deliver and the others know what to expect. In the words of Don Sull and Charles Spinosa, these "explicit promises clear the fog of anonymity that surrounds collective commitments made to abstract goals like 'capturing synergies' or 'filling the white spaces.' When the 'who', 'what,' and 'to whom' are explicit, commitments leave little place to hide."

Making motivated commitments

Commitments hold when they are motivated through the conversation that takes place between the person who has made a request and the person who has committed to action. It is during these conversations that a clearer understanding of the request emerges and that acceptance of the commitment occurs. The most effective commitments are grounded in a shared understanding of what is important for the goals of the Hot Spot. By linking the specific to the general, we align our action to the actions of others in the Hot Spot.

Practice 3: Resolving Conflicts

Perhaps surprisingly, my research revealed few differences in terms of conflict between Hot Spots that persisted and those that dissipated. In all Hot Spots there is conflict about what each person could contribute, about the purpose of the Hot Spot, and about its pace and schedules. In fact, I found that often this conflict generated the energy needed to solve problems. Without any form of conflict, a potentially vibrant Hot Spot can rapidly depreciate into a tepid "country club."[2]

Conflict was present in all the Hot Spots we studied. The difference between Hot Spots that flourished and those that became cold was the way in which this conflict was faced up to and resolved. There are many possible areas of conflict in Hot Spots: disputes about the goals and what people are actually trying to achieve; conflicts of interests about the pacing and schedule, with some individuals wishing to go faster than others; and disagreements about the resource implications, with some people overstating or understating the resources required. There can even be conflicts regarding the outcome criteria, how people will know whether they have been successful.

So even though the quantity of potential conflicts was similar, Hot Spots that flourish have developed means to maximize the creative tension of conflicts. They do this in three ways. First, members of the Hot Spot find ways to acknowledge, surface, and discuss tensions and conflicts as they arise. This is what Richard Pascale calls "uncompromising straight talk." He believes that conflict reframed as organizational learning can be crucial to the organization's long-term vitality.[3] In other words, the resolution of conflict is built into the day-to-day norms of behavior. Next, there is sufficient courage within the group to face up to challenges and resolve conflicts by reference to the performance outcomes. Finally, people in productive Hot Spots confront conflict by making and keeping commitments.

However, the creation of the "prevailing temporal agenda" is no easy matter. In fact, we discovered that the most frequent sources of conflict in Hot Spots were two aspects of the use of time: individual pacing preferences and the synchronization of work. To come to terms with conflicts regarding time, members of Hot Spots have to learn the art of synchronizing time.

Practice 4: Synchronizing Time

Time matters in Hot Spots.[4] Each Hot Spot has its own rhythm, tempo, and pace. This unique temporal structure reflects the profound individual and cultural differences among members of a Hot Spot with regard to perceptions of time and timing preferences. Unresolved, these individual and cultural differences can become some of the most crucial freezers of Hot Spots. They represent a distinct and what can be almost insurmountable barrier to Hot Spot productivity. Conflicts of time are most often resolved through the use of explicit schedules and the sequencing of deadlines to coordinate activities. This solution also calls on the ability of members of the Hot Spot to adjust the phasing of their behavior to align with others.[5]

Much of the conflict around time arises as a result of personality differences and the complexity of working across time zones. Type A characters enjoy the adrenaline rush of tight schedules and actively seek to create this type of high-pressure working environment. Others with slower time preferences find this irritating and perplexing. So when conflicts around time are to be resolved, some acknowledgment of individual differences is essential.

When Hot Spots flourish in the long run, they do so through flexibility, feedback, and synchronization.

Synchronizing time through flexibility

In Hot Spots adept at synchronizing time, there is much flexibility. Some are flexible around the pacing of activities, speeding up or slowing down as necessary. Some are flexible with regard to the timing of activities. Finally, there is flexibility around the timing of activity bundles, that is, the degree to which parts of the activities can be combined or separated. Flexibility occurs when the task is split into units of activities of different size that can be done in the time available. This modular approach to activities and tasks is reminiscent of the flexibility of Nokia's signature modular architecture.

Technology is crucial to the synchronization of time in Hot Spots, particularly when they span time zones. This technology typically uses both *synchronous* and *asynchronous communication.* Synchronous communication is crucial at the beginning of a Hot Spot when people are becoming acquainted with each other and appreciative of each other's talents. Typically, members of these productive Hot Spots make extensive use of teleconferencing and videoconferencing at early stages. They also begin to make extensive use of asynchronous communication such as Web sites and blogs on which people post their views and ideas at times convenient for them. This asynchronous communication allows participants in a Hot Spot greater personal flexibility in terms of time and activity.

Productive Hot Spots abound with flexibility. They also abound with feedback that helps the Hot Spot continue to sizzle, despite the complexity of time.

Synchronizing time through feedback

Timing almost always changes over the course of a Hot Spot. This is to be expected, given the complexities of interdependence between people and the evolving nature of the purpose of the Hot Spot. Sometimes schedules shorten when events move faster than anticipated; sometimes schedules are delayed when events move more slowly. In Hot Spots that are poorly maintained, these unpredictable changes in timing can have the effect of calling in the Big Freeze. Most people haven't much tolerance for repeated and unpredictable changes in schedule. Yet in Hot Spots, speed-ups and especially delays are inevitable.

The challenge for Hot Spots, then, is to reduce as much as possible the negative feelings associated with schedule changes. Psychoanalysts and psychologists have documented human impatience when things are delayed. However, there are circumstances when we are less impatient and frustrated with schedule changes. In productive Hot Spots, there are many ways in which impatience and frustration can be minimized.

One effective way is simply to cultivate the expectation that changes may occur. This becomes a topic of conversation at a relatively early stage, and this *heedful interaction* continues throughout the life span of the Hot Spot. Next, speed-ups or delays are less frustrating when the opportunity costs are not significantly high. For example, the groups should not agree to a high-profile event that, if it were to be rescheduled, would result in a great loss of face. Finally, delays are less likely to be frustrating when members have other activities that they can set aside during a speed-up or to which they can turn during a delay.[6]

Synchronizing time through socialization and pacing

When Hot Spots emerge across a single time zone, the challenge is primarily one of flexibility and feedback. This can be achieved through flexible schedules that allow participants some timing freedom and that provide sufficient feedback that people are able to adjust their timing and scheduling. However, when Hot Spots arise across time zones, synchronizing time becomes far more complex. Take Pertti and Huang at Nokia, for example.

Their attempts to synchronize across time zones will inevitably raise issues of individual differences in schedule flexibility and timing.

To maintain the Hot Spot at Nokia, Pertti and Huang and the others have to fine-tune the art of synchronization. This will involve synchronizing their personal perceptions of time as well as their activities and tasks. Because they work in different time zones, they have to become adept at "crossing time."[7]

An initial appreciation of talents and working styles is crucial to this. Each participant in a Hot Spot is carrying what we might call "time baggage," previous knowledge, habits, and expectations about time. Some of this will be explicit—for example, the way the person likes to schedule work. More of it will be implicit—for example, how time is perceived. What may be "fast" in one zone may be "too fast" in another or "too slow" in a third.

For Pertti and Huang, synchronizing their personal perspectives on time is important right at the start. They then have to synchronize the phasing and rhythm of their work. Think of this synchronization of pacing as analogous to the tuning fork. The tuning fork is set at a given pitch, and when it is set in motion and placed near another stationary fork of the same frequency, it will begin vibrating more or less in synchrony with the first. In the same way, to synchronize across time, we need to attune our activities to each other. Synchronization also has analogies in the natural world. Consider the circadian rhythms, the changes that occur in all living things over the course of a twenty-four-hour day. All animals and plants have physiological and biological processes that operate in rhythmic, periodic, or oscillating forms. Under normal conditions of life on earth, these processes begin to shift phases and frequency and become what biologists refer to as entrained to one another. Typically, these operate as a bundle of biological processes over a period of twenty-four hours in synchrony with day and night and the rotation of the planet. When conditions change, these "free-running" rhythms shift to periodicities near, but not exactly at, the day-night twenty-four-hour interval.[8]

Both Pertti and Huang are familiar with circadian rhythms. When Pertti steps off the plane from Helsinki to Beijing, his body rhythms are still operating on Finnish time. The discomfort he feels—what we generally refer to as "jet lag"—is the result of the decoupling of his body's rhythms from the circadian bundle. Over a period of a week, his body will adjust to the new night-and-day periodicity, and he will become more lively and energetic. In reality, of course, he is back on the plane to Helsinki before that period of adjustment, to return with a new case of jet lag.

For Hot Spots to flourish across time zones, the same sort of synchronization has to occur. In the natural world, the synchronization of pacing involves both the rhythms of the separate processes that make up the circadian bundle and synchronization to a powerful external signal or force, the *zeitgebers,* or "time givers." When Pertti is eventually able to get over the discomfort of jet lag and synchronize his sleep pattern to day and night in China, it is because of light and temperature signals his brain receives. The pace of these signals enables his body to adjust to the new day-night cycle—to reset his "internal clock." That is, by the way, why his doctor recommends that as soon as he lands in China, he should go into the bright sunshine or a bright room.

For Pertti and Huang to synchronize their work over the coming months, they too need powerful external forces. The most obvious external force will be schedules and task deadlines. Synchronization around task deadlines can have a positive impact on the productivity and innovation of the Hot Spot. They can also have a negative impact. Imagine for a moment that the two teams become synchronized into meeting stringent deadlines. With this shared temporal framework, they are likely to go straight into the execution stage of the work and eliminate virtually all the crucial first stages of appreciating talents and making commitments. Synchronization that proceeds at too fast a pace is likely to be detrimental to the Hot Spot. Slower synchronization increases the likelihood of producing greater value in the long term.

Technology plays a crucial role in the synchronization of pacing. When people such as Pertti and Huang are operating in time zones with an eight-hour difference, finding "together" time can be tricky. One way of dealing with this is to create what have been called "temporal boundary objects."[9] These create links across temporal voids. Deborah Ancona gives the example of the patient chart.[10] This allows doctors and nurses who work on different shifts and schedules and have differing time preferences to relay information to one another and to continue patient care without interruption.

Temporal boundary objects can take various forms in Hot Spots. They can be, for example, the shared space in a chat room, which anyone can access at any time to add ideas and comments. It can take the form of a shared project schedule that defines the aim of each person's work and the progress being made. This enables more fluid communication and planning across temporal zones.

To understand this use of technology in synchronizing time, let's take a closer look at the Nokia team. For the first hour that Pertti and his colleagues sit across the table at headquarters in Finland to discuss the problems in Asia, they are engaged in face-to-face communication with no intermediating technology. Everyone is an independent source of input, and all are party to the input of every other member. All are in the same place at the same time, all are known to each other, and the person who is speaking is known. They are members of a full and open communication network. In that case, there are norms of meetings that we might expect to see. We might expect a relatively orderly distribution of participation over time and few interruptions or times when more than one person is speaking. We would also expect everyone to participate about equally, with the highest-status person in the room, the CEO, perhaps talking somewhat more.

When Pertti begins to talk with Huang over the coming weeks, the teams communicate electronically. They use technologies such as videoconferencing, telephone conferencing, and online computer conferencing to span the distance between them. These synchronizing technologies enable them to coordinate their time and actions. They also use technologies such as asynchronous computer conferencing and e-mail that enable them to bridge time.

We might expect that in the first week of the project, a stream of e-mail would crisscross the ever-expanding network of people involved in the project. In these e-mail communications, we can observe a change from the implicit communication regulations we saw in the face-to-face meeting in Helsinki. For example, there is likely to be more equal participation regardless of status.[11] This means, in effect, that many more people will contribute, but not necessarily because they have something worthwhile to contribute. There is also likely to be a much less orderly and more chaotic flow of inputs over time. There are more anomalies in the succession of speakers. There may be delays in participation and longer and less predictable lags between inputs and feedback. Without establishing an etiquette or protocol for e-mail, Pertti and his colleagues will find themselves overwhelmed with e-mail either addressed or forwarded to them.

As the project develops, Pertti and his team make more and more use of computer conferencing in real time. This is most useful when signature systems are used to identify contributors, when participants agree to read and react to contributions within a certain time frame, and when minimum and maximum levels of input by each participant have been set. The issue here is less the development of hardware and more the establishment of social contracts among the participants. These agreements come close to re-creating the kinds of social norms that arise spontaneously in face-to-face communication settings.

◐ Practice 5: Establishing a Rhythm

As Hot Spots heat up, the challenge of time moves from synchronization to rhythm. Increasingly, participants in Hot Spot begin to suffer from a lack of time for reflection. As they rely more and more on schedules and time-keeping, reflection time gets lost. Any excess time is viewed as "slack" and is quickly filled. Time becomes a commodity to be allocated and exploited.

There are times in Hot Spots when reflection must take place. Sally, one of the members of a cross–time zone Hot Spot, helped me to understand this better. In conversation about Hot Spots, this is what she told me: "My daily work life is filled with schedules and meetings. I always seem to be behind, always in a rush. When I am engaged within this, it feels different. Although we don't spend that much time actually together or in communication, it seems that these are really important hours. It feels like every moment counts."

Sally was reflecting on a difference in time that ancient Greeks understood: *Chronos,* the length of time, and *kairos,* the activities that occur in that space of time. Chronos is clock time, time abstracted from the relation to personal action, time, as it were, that clicks on objectively and impersonally whether anything is happening or not. It is time measured by the chronometer, not the purpose, momentary rather than momentous. The word *kairos* derives from the Greek deity Kairos, the youngest son of Zeus and the god of opportunity. It is related to the word *kinesis,* meaning movement, change, and the emergence of the new and active innovation. *Kairos* can be the defining moment. It is subjective time, time considered in relation to personal action, in reference to the ends achieved in it.

Sally, like all of us at one time or another, was reflecting on the fact that although clock time, *chronos,* may be shorter in Hot Spots, her experience of it in terms of the impact it has on her—that is, *kairos,* feels longer. Intuitively, she has made the same distinction in her mind. The distinction is an important one, we found; when people describe their experiences in Hot Spots, they say they seem to achieve more and every second seems to count. This is the effect of focusing on timelessness and their own intrinsic motivation.

Focus on timelessness

In productive Hot Spots, there is dexterity with regard to time. There is *chronos* in the synchronization of schedules and planning meetings. There is also *kairos,* where the emphasis is on the quality of time rather than the quantity of time, the intensity rather than the duration and frequency, the extension of time rather than the compression of time, and the circular nature of time rather than the linear perception of time. As the philosopher Elliot Jacques points out, synchronizing through our watches is easy; we can agree on the temporal sequences and time frames. But synchronizing the flow of our respective intentions is much more difficult to achieve.[12]

And yet in great Hot Spots, this synchronization of time seems to occur. My colleague at London Business School, Babis Mainemelis, has made a life's work around studying what he calls "times of timelessness."[13] He has discovered that there are certain situations and times when people are more likely to experience timelessness. Timelessness most often occurs when we are totally absorbed in a task. This has important implications for the design of office space and the opportunity for people to work at home—if they find home a place of peace and tranquility. Recall how David Ogilvy, the founder of OgilvyOne, used his châteaux as a place of reflection, and this habit continues into the present at OgilvyOne with the use of quiet rooms that people can go to separately or together.

As people enter a period of timelessness, they often do so with some kind of rite of passage. This could be a brief habitual activity or ritual that promotes psychological and physical engagement with the task—for example, arranging one's desk in a certain way or sharpening a pencil. For groups, this may be the ritual of listening to each person in turn to catch up on events. These small rituals serve to attract attention away from the surrounding organization and increase emotional arousal.

Once settled, individuals and groups experience timelessness when there is a clear goal in which they are engaged. The goal itself is not important. What is important is that the goal helps people know what they are working toward and gives them a target. Focus on a goal is particularly crucial to prevent people from surrendering to a variety of potential distractions. The factor that Babis Mainemelis found is critical to this state of timelessness is the balance between the challenge of the task and person's own skill level.[14] When our skills exceed the challenge of the task, the activity becomes boring, and we begin to lose interest and motivation. When the goal is too difficult, we become frustrated and anxious. Activities that balance challenges and skills excite our interest and ensure that attention is focused on the activity.

The challenge for Hot Spots and timelessness is that the very activity of cooperation can hinder timelessness. We are constantly interrupted by our colleagues, and their work times and deadlines put us into a state of anxiety and distraction, so we end up responding to their work rhythms rather than listening to our own.[15] These distractions can have a detrimental impact on our capacity to move into timelessness. However, I discovered that certain people do find a way to be part of a Hot Spot and yet experience timelessness. Those who move into timelessness have typically developed the habit of intrinsic motivation.

Intrinsic motivation

People who achieve timelessness in Hot Spots have developed the habit of only working on tasks that they really enjoy—that they find intrinsically motivating. They shun tasks that they know they would not enjoy or that others foist on them. Often these intrinsically motivating tasks are ones that are inherently satisfying rather than done only to obtain some outcome separate from the activity.[16]

Finding tasks and experiences that are intrinsically motivating sounds relatively straightforward, but in fact it requires a heightened awareness of who we are. Without this emotional self-awareness, we have no capacity to judge whether the tasks available to us could be intrinsically motivating. With emotional self-awareness, we are able to accurately assess our own internal states, resources, and limitations. By doing so, we are able to prepare ourselves for becoming engaged both rationally and emotionally in the task.[17]

Finding intrinsically motivating tasks also requires the companies of which we are members to communicate the tasks available and to encourage volunteering. Recall how the energy around the BT Hot Spots arose in part because people knew what the goal was and could volunteer to join teams working on a subject they found intrinsically motivating. When we are assigned tasks and have little choice, we are much less likely to discover aspects of our work that we would find intrinsically motivating.

In Hot Spots where timelessness flourishes, people have learned how to create and protect a space in their workday or workweek for experiencing timelessness. Over time, they have become more and more adept at creating more opportunities to become engrossed in work. In this way, they reinforce the cycle of working in a context that is intrinsically motivating and conducive to creativity. This pleasure in turn creates more passion, persistence, and perseverance in developing and carrying out creative tasks.

The combination of the four elements of a Hot Spot—cooperative mindset, boundary spanning, igniting purpose, and productive capacity—creates a context in which there is a significant chance of Hot Spots emerging. Let us now return to one of the questions posed at the very beginning. If Hot Spots are indeed emergent phenomena, what, if anything, can executives do to encourage their emergence? This is the question that frames the following chapter.

CHAPTER SUMMARY

PRODUCTIVE CAPACITY

Key Points

The latent energy of Hot Spots, fueled by a mindset of cooperation and boundary spanning, are ignited with purpose. However, for Hot Spots to be productive, this energy has to be channeled through five productive processes:

- Appreciating the talents of the people in the Hot Spot

- Making public commitments about one's own contribution

- Resolving the conflicts that emerge within the Hot Spot

- Synchronizing time when people have different time frames or are operating in different time zones

- Establishing a rhythm that ensures that times of frenetic activity are interspersed with times of reflection and timelessness

New Rules

- **Commitments.** Hot Spots are formed at the nexus of a network of commitments that establish what actions will be taken and by whom. The responsibility of participants in a Hot Spot is to make and keep public, voluntary, and explicit commitments.

- **Rhythm and timelessness.** A Hot Spot involves periods of intense activity that fuels the productive capacity of the Hot Spot. The creative output of a Hot Spot is fueled by times of reflection and timelessness. Without this temporal aspect, the Hot Spot burns out and suboptimizes the creative endeavor.

7

THE LEADER'S ROLE IN HOT SPOTS

> Hot Spots = (Cooperative Mindset x Boundary Spanning x Igniting Purpose) x Productive Capacity

I F HOT SPOTS ARE EMERGENT rather than controlled and directed, what can the role of the leader be? The old rules of command and control will have little effect on Hot Spots and may actually work against their emergence. In companies with more than their fair share of Hot Spots, my research colleagues and I found that leaders had played a crucial role by asking the difficult igniting questions, creating a network of friendships and opportunities for boundaryless cooperation, and championing and supporting the unique signature processes that create the context for the emergence of Hot Spots.

◘ Leader as Socrates

There are leaders in Hot Spot–rich companies whose vision of the future is so enticing that it results in the almost instantaneous release of latent energy. The founders of Wikipedia and Linux were able to galvanize thousands of volunteers with the promise of knowledge for all and the idea of an open system platform, respectively. Not all leaders have this all-encompassing vision of the future. What they do have is big questions. In their own way, they are latter-day versions of Socrates.

The ancient philosopher Socrates established the utility of asking big questions of ordinary people he met as he walked the streets of Athens. Socrates used these conversations to analyze the issues of the day and his own ideas. He was convinced that people might be wrong, even when they held important positions and when they were espousing beliefs held for centuries by vast majorities of people. The reason was simple: they had not examined their beliefs logically.

In his own practice of questioning, Socrates established that while there is value in finding affirmation for existing assumptions and beliefs, the most useful learning occurs through falsification. Falsification requires the discipline of reason and hypothesis testing. What are the assumptions behind this proposal? What data or evidence would we need to prove those assumptions to be false? What do we believe to be true that is actually untrue? What do we believe to be untrue that is actually true? These were the types of questions Socrates asked, and they provide the foundation for rigorous, rational conversations and guide leaders toward potential igniting questions.

A Hot Spot needs a leader like Socrates as a source of vigorous and disciplined questioning. At BP, John Browne personally embodies this belief in rigor and rationality. "Rigor implies that you understand the assumptions you have made," he said, "assumptions about the state of the world, what you can do, and how your competitors will react, and how the policies of the world will or will not allow you to do something." He regularly takes his top team through intellectually challenging inquiries. Could the price of oil drop below $10 a barrel in the medium term? It's unlikely, but what happens if it does? How will technical substitution work in the short term? "The main point is that we keep interrogating and asking questions about these things, and that ensures that others in the organization will do so too," says Browne.

Most companies have developed an internal environment in which any form of doubt is perceived as ignorance or weakness and all forms of questioning are interpreted as either manipulation or affront. It is this delegitimization of questioning and doubt that kills the spirit of inquiry and reduces conversations to ritualized, dehydrated talk. The first task of the leader in creating good conversations is to institutionalize questioning and expressing doubt as a normal and routine part of the way in which the company operates.

Although systems such as scenario planning can help people in companies overcome the constant need to project an aura of certainty, the most important power for legitimizing questioning and expressions of doubt lies in the personal influence of top-level leaders. This will perhaps be John Browne's most important legacy at BP: long after the novelty of acquisitions and industry restructuring have faded into footnotes of BP's history, his ability to convert the ritualized, bureaucratic norms of interactions within the company into an environment of constant vigorous yet courteous questioning and inquiry will be remembered.

The ability to ask incisive questions requires careful cultivation. Spotting potential weaknesses or fallacies in an argument is a bit like exploiting good luck; both need prepared minds. To be effective questioners, top-level leaders need to constantly expose themselves to a variety of information and stimuli inside and outside the company so as to be able to generate independent and insightful thoughts.

This is precisely what Browne and his top-level colleagues at BP have done. They have all built individual links with faculty members in high-quality universities—Cambridge, Stanford, Yale—and a variety of experts in other institutions and regularly visit them "to keep in touch with people who know more than we do," in the words of Nick Butler, BP's policy adviser. Browne himself uses his board positions at Intel and Goldman Sachs to gain new insights into industry models. Discussions on the Intel board are precisely what encouraged him to question BP's IT investment plans and to avoid overinvestment in new systems, even though the company looked old-fashioned at the time.

The risk, however, is that constant questioning would lead to a highly politicized environment of second guessing and point scoring. The antidote to that risk is a relentless focus on purpose. It is the focus on goals that converts great questions into effective learning. "You can implore people to learn," said Browne, "and they will, to some extent. But if you say, 'Look, the learning is necessary in order to cut the cost of drilling a well by 10 percent,' then they will learn with a purpose."

To legitimize honest expressions of doubt, leaders need to admit their own doubts and uncertainties. Underlying Socrates' ability to question was his belief that he knew nothing. Top managers who believe that they must always have the right answers kill curiosity and inquiry. It takes a lot of self-confidence and courage for leaders to acknowledge their own ignorance, but nothing serves as a better reminder to others of all the things that they themselves do not know. Authenticity in human relationships almost inevitably requires reciprocal expression of vulnerabilities and weaknesses, and leaders expressing honest doubts provide a key foundation for developing authenticity in organizations.

So one of the key tasks of leaders who want to encourage Hot Spots is to authentically shape the conversational agenda in their companies. Of course, routine must be dealt with and urgencies must be tackled. But great leaders always ensure that the day-to-day pragmatics do not take over the entire conversational space for employees. They keep in play a few broad questions to engage the intellect and the imagination of their people. Great conversations around those topics not only translate into concrete here-and-now benefits but also constantly renew the identity of the institution and the bonds among people and between them and the company.

In his very first meeting with senior managers after taking over as the CEO of IBM, Lou Gerstner made a new rule: no overhead projectors and no slides will be allowed into the room. In IBM, meetings had become totally ritualized, with formal presentations of information using well-crafted color slides. Managers spent an enormous amount of time preparing these presentations, which took up all the available time during the meetings. Instead of fancy presentations, Gerstner wanted quality conversations. Hence his new rule: no slides.

James Houghton, at the time the CEO of Corning, made a similar rule. Anyone who believed that he or she would add or receive nothing of value at a particular meeting could remove his or her name from the list of participants for that meeting. A very large number of ritualized meetings died very quickly.

Imposing another rule, a department manager at Sun Microsystems set a bunch of small black flags in his meeting room. Whenever a participant believed that someone was preventing a good conversation in any way, the participant could hold up a flag for all to see. It took a while for people to develop the confidence and comfort to use the flags, but once they did, the quality of conversations rapidly improved.

Individual habits and organizational inertia lead to the persistence of poor conversations in companies. Most leaders can think of any number of such simple rules that break habits and inertia. The actual rule needs to be adjusted to the historical and cultural context of the company; what matters is that the leaders consciously ask the questions: What is blocking quality conversations in our organization? What can we do to eliminate the blockages? Once the questions are asked, some creative and insightful instrument for breaking old habits inevitably emerges.

Similarly, creating new forums is often a powerful way to redirect conversations in companies. Established forums get institutionalized over time, and it becomes increasingly difficult to change the patterns of conversations that occur in those forums. In new forums, new patterns can be established, among new participants.

Leader as the Creator of Friendships

I remember being very struck by a conversation with Rory Sutherland, the creative director of OgilvyOne. His point was this: "The most important role of the manager at OgilvyOne is to create friendships." This was at the very beginning of the Hot Spot research, and frankly, at the time, I thought this was rather extreme. *Friendship* is not a word you hear much around companies. Yet over the intervening period, I have warmed more and more to his view. It is clear to me that this job of creating friendships is crucial to the emergence of Hot Spots.

It begins with the quality and depth of relationships the members of the leadership team have with each other. Poor-quality relationships have a profoundly negative effect on the capacity of the company to thrive. But more than this, they send out strong messages to the other members of the organization about what is legitimate and what is not.

Sometimes these friendships require real courage on the part of the leader. While OgilvyOne under the direction of its founder, David Ogilvy, had been a friendly place, by 1992 its original entrepreneurial culture had ossified into highly autonomous factions led by barons who were more interested in protecting their turf than in building the business. "The London office was horrible," a senior manager told me, "with constant backbiting and a lot of bad blood."

The change started with Charlotte Beers, the then CEO of Ogilvy, who invited all the business leaders to a two-day off-site meeting. Breaking with norms, she began the conversation by asking direct questions: "How do we feel about one another? Why can't we work together? Do we recognize what that is doing to our clients?" That meeting was the turning point. Initially, the discussions were very difficult. "We simply did not know how to talk openly to each other," the same senior manager told us. "We were so used to being defensive and polite. It took two years and eight meetings—and some changes in the cast of characters—before we learned to deal with emotions and feelings, to be authentic. Its only through that process that we learned the power of friendship."

Leader as the Architect of Signature Processes

Hot Spots emerge; they cannot be ordered to appear. However, their presence and longevity are highly influenced by the context of the company, in particular its practices and processes. I have suggested a whole portfolio of practices and processes that will make a significant impact on the probability of Hot Spots emerging. Selecting cooperative people, broadening socialization and induction, and engaging in activities that encourage a feeling of community are just a few of the wide range of potential leverage points. Much of the responsibility for the design and delivery of these practices and processes can be taken by members of the human resource function.

However, in each company, there are a handful of practices and processes that leaders must personally involve themselves with, ones that are unique to the company. These are not best practices imported from elsewhere; rather they are the practices and processes that resonate with the values of the company. These are signature processes, and leaders play a crucial role in defining and sponsoring them.

At the heart of signature processes such as peer assist at BP, the modular architecture at Nokia, the selection process at Goldman Sachs, and the Challenge Cup at BT are the CEOs and their teams. In each of these companies, the CEO believes that the signature process in question is key to the organization's long-term success, and each is committed to maintaining the signature process. By putting resources and commitment behind these signature practices, these leaders support the spontaneous development of Hot Spots. What can other executives learn from these companies?

Most executives know that values are important in their day-to-day behavior; few understand that it is through a small number of signature processes that these values can be integrated into the goals of the business and the behaviors of individual employees. What I learned from leaders such as John Browne at BP and Jorma Ollila at Nokia is that these exceptional leaders use signature processes as a means to communicate their values and the values of the company. To do so requires that the leader be very clear about what those values are.

The executive role in identifying externally developed best practices is essentially rational and analytical; in contrast, the executive role in signature processes is value-based and insightful. I could hear the pride in senior executive Mikko Kosonen's voice when he talked of Nokia's modular structure: "One of the distinctive characteristics of Nokia is the organizational architecture. It is avant-garde." Over hours of discussions, Nokia executives tried to describe the structure, their ideas behind it, how it worked, and what it meant. Figures were drawn, analogies made, and examples given— all with enthusiasm and caring. And at BP, there is a huge amount of pride in the philosophy that underpins the peer assist process. As Deputy CEO Rodney Chase remarked, "In our personal lives, we all know how much joy we derive from helping others. As a mother, a brother, or a friend, we derive great pleasure from helping those who are close to become successful. Why don't we believe that the same can be true in business? Historically, we didn't. But you can get there when people in the company can almost derive more pleasure from the success of others than from their own success."

We saw that when people are participating in the signature processes, they are "in the flow." The energy they exhibit is palpable, and they are oblivious to time. When people participate in these signature processes, they feel good precisely because, deep down, the process expresses something they believe in. They feel that what they are doing deeply resonates with who they are and what they value.

Executives know exactly what they have to do to build best-practice processes. They have to approach the task with rigor and a clear time frame in mind. These characteristics are not useful to the executive in the creation of signature processes, which are at their core value-driven. The creation of signature processes is more serendipitous and is by its nature slower, more complex, and more expressive of values.

These executives have learned that like values, signature processes can be ephemeral. They understand that describing, protecting, and engaging in signature processes is one of the most valuable opportunities they have to live up to their company's values. These executives feel passionate about these processes because they understand that day-to-day activities can be a crucial link between the goals of the business and its values. As a result, signature processes are potentially energizing and can bring meaning in a way that best practices never can.

◎ Points of Inflection

The real challenge for executives is that many of them are leading companies which are themselves at a point of inflection. This point of inflection occurs when what has served well in the past will not serve well in the future. The two curves are illustrated in Figure 7.1. The characteristics of the first curve have been developed and honed over the last century. In a sense they illustrate the current rules of managing people in businesses. These rules have served us well. Many companies reached their current performance precisely because they concentrated on the rules of productivity and the leader operated as the central control figure of the company. The emphasis was on creating schedules and importing best practice from other companies. The practices and processes of the company focused on the selection, rewarding and development of individuals who were managed through rules, procedures and directives. The challenge with these rules is that many of them will be less appropriate as companies become more global, more complex, and more innovative. In fact, as the curve illustrates, there will be a time when these rules actually begin to work against the performance of the company.

The challenge for leaders is that to move into the next curve of value creation requires them to be making significant changes, even as the first curve seems to be the most appropriate. To take on a whole new set of rules—even as the current rules appear appropriate. As the second curve of Figure 7.1, illustrates the rules are beginning to change. Increasingly value in a company will be created less through incremental productivity improvements, and more through innovation through new combinations. The role of leader will be less about controlling and commanding, and more about igniting energy and enabling groups to volunteer and emerge. Where schedules have dominated there has to be a stronger emphasis on rhythm and timelessness. In the first curve the role of the leader was as supporter of the importation of best practice. In the second curve it is as the champion of signature processes.

Where the emphasis in the first curve is on individuals, in the second curve it is groups and the relationships and networks between them that

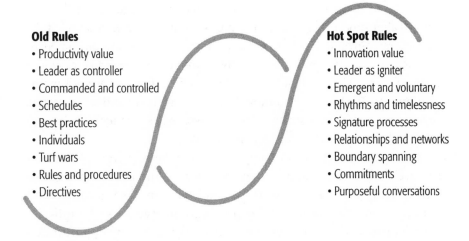

Old Rules
- Productivity value
- Leader as controller
- Commanded and controlled
- Schedules
- Best practices
- Individuals
- Turf wars
- Rules and procedures
- Directives

Hot Spot Rules
- Innovation value
- Leader as igniter
- Emergent and voluntary
- Rhythms and timelessness
- Signature processes
- Relationships and networks
- Boundary spanning
- Commitments
- Purposeful conversations

Figure 7.1 Points of inflection in organizations: shifting from old rules to new

will assume ever greater importance. The second curve is less about rules and procedures, and more about commitments and conversations.

Many companies are beginning to approach the apex of the first curve, when simply doing more of the same is not increasing the value of their company. To do so they will have to abandon some of the old rules, and begin to build competence and energy around the new rules of the second curve. Those that fail to do so will see a gradual but consistent decline in the capacity to create value.

At the heart of the second curve are the rules of Hot Spots—the idea that energy can be ignited, that relationships and networks are crucial, that commitments and conversations can replace rules and directives.

This is no easy challenge. As leaders and members of organizations, we often find ourselves at a point of inflection. What worked in the past is not working so well anymore. The context in which we work has changed fundamentally as technology joins up the world and globalization opens up new markets for capital, talent, products, and services. We see this in the Hot Spots we observed earlier. Recall how technology has enabled Amit to converse with Linux colleagues around the world free of charge. Consider how the globalization of telecoms has meant that within the Hot Spot that links Finland and China, an executive like Pertti needs to know as much about the buying habits of fourteen-year-olds in China as he does about the buying habits of the children in his own country.

We are all at a point of inflection as the nature of working together has changed almost beyond recognition. At this point of inflection, some of the old rules remain, and these can act as barriers to change and ultimately to the emergence of Hot Spots. Yet simply getting rid of the old rules would create a free-for-all. The Hot Spots at Linux and Wikipedia are not manifestations of anarchy. In fact, although they are emergent and self-directed, they are also highly orchestrated. Each has evolved its own identity, its own norms of behavior, and its own ways of working.

The mistake would be for companies to see these emerging Hot Spots as entirely self-directed and anarchistic. There is still a place for routine work and formal work groups. Yet as you have seen, the innovation and value creation of Hot Spots will increasingly emerge across boundaries where individuals have choices regarding participation and opportunities to indulge their passion and volunteer their knowledge.

Hot Spots are not amenable to the old rules of command and control, under which employees are told what to do and then rewarded for their actions. In the new rules of Hot Spots, rather than be commanded, employees choose to develop important relationships with others, and rather than be controlled, they actively choose to make their time available to this collective sense of purpose.

The Rules of a Hot Spot

Leaders can play a crucial role in creating a context in which Hot Spots can emerge. To do so requires them to move to the second curve in Figure 7.1—to replace some of the old ways of working with new rules. As we have progressed through the four elements of a Hot Spot, we have considered the new rules associated with each one of these elements. Let us now review all nine new rules.

- **Value creation.** Value within companies is created by exploiting what is already known through strong bonds. Novelty and innovation emerge through exploration, facilitated by relationships and network of relationships that cross boundaries. Be absolutely aware of what is appropriate and where, and design networks around this.

- **Ignition and leadership.** The latent energy in boundaryless cooperation is ignited with a spark. It could be the spark of a compelling vision, the stimulus of a question, or the excitement of a complex and meaningful task. The responsibility of the leader is to ensure that this spark is created.

- **Emergence.** Hot Spots emerge; they cannot be ordered forth or directed. People choose freely to give of their human capital (intellectual, emotional, or social), or they volunteer.

- **Rhythm and timelessness.** A Hot Spot is marked by periods of intense activity that fuel its productive capacity. The creative output of a Hot Spot is fueled by times of reflection and timelessness. Without these moments, the Hot Spot burns out and suboptimizes the creative endeavor.

- **Signature processes.** Much can be done to create an environment in which boundaryless cooperation will emerge. However, although the importation of best practices is important, it is not sufficient. The new rule is to move beyond best practices to signature processes.

- **Relationships.** The value of Hot Spots is created in the space between people. Hot Spots are fundamentally relational, whether the relationship is between close friends or acquaintances. The new rule is that the focus of resources with regard to support and development needs to be on the individual and on the network of relationships.

- **Boundary spanners.** Hot Spots become moribund without boundary spanners, who bring insights from outside the Hot Spot group. But the role is complex and at times distracting. Be committed to boundary spanners; nurture and cherish them.

- **Commitments.** Hot Spots are formed at the nexus of a network of commitments that establish what actions will be taken and by whom. The responsibility of Hot Spot participants is to make and keep the commitments public, voluntary, and explicit.

- **Purposeful conversation.** Conversation is the source of igniting purpose. Support and shape conversation with insightful data, an emphasis on values, and space for reflection.

Much of our way of thinking about the role of management has centered on the rules of command and control. Supporting the emergence of Hot Spots requires a whole new set of rules and a whole new way of approaching the challenge. To take a mechanistic approach to the emergence of Hot Spots is to entirely miss the point of their development. This does not mean that nothing can be done, but it takes a more subtle, more nuanced, and I believe more sophisticated approach. It requires unlearning some of the old rules and learning a whole new set of rules. Executives who create a space where Hot Spots can emerge live by the rules of Hot Spots, and employees act and behave by them.

These new rules require a rather different way of thinking about the creation of value in organizations. These new rules invite us to change our conceptions of organizations and some of our underlying assumptions. They challenge our thinking about practices and habits of behavior. We cannot order Hot Spots to emerge, but we can create an environment in which the probability of their emergence is significantly increased. Leaders can take an active role in championing and supporting Hot Spots, and employees can strive to adopt a mindset of cooperation and act as boundary spanners.

Enabling the emergence of Hot Spots is essentially about context and leadership behaviors. The challenge is knowing where to start, knowing what aspects of the context and behaviors to change and what aspects to retain. It is to this challenge that we turn in Chapter 8.

CHAPTER SUMMARY

THE LEADERS' ROLE IN HOT SPOTS

Key Points

In companies with more than their fair share of Hot Spots, leaders play a crucial role.

- **Leader as Socrates.** Leaders need the courage and confidence to ask the hard questions, to see old problems in new ways, and to use rigor and discipline to get to the heart of issues.

- **Leader as the creator of friendships.** Leaders need to stimulate the creation of personal networks and friendships that encourage others to value the relational element of the organization and the maintenance of networks within and beyond the company.

- **Leader as architect of signature processes.** Leaders need to champion organizational practices that resonate with the values of the company and their own personal beliefs and vision.

8

DESIGNING FOR THE EMERGENCE OF HOT SPOTS

> *Hot Spots = (Cooperative Mindset x Boundary Spanning x Igniting Purpose) x Productive Capacity*

H OT SPOTS ARE CRUCIAL to organizational health. They are the energy that fuels constant performance improvements and the source of breakthrough innovations. Without the energy and focus of Hot Spots, companies languish and die. Yet Hot Spots pose a real challenge for executives and organizations as we attempt to craft and develop them. We can design for the emergence of Hot Spots, and to do so requires thought, insight, and courage. This chapter takes a closer look at how we can align the company to the emergence of Hot Spots and consider the tools and techniques most able to help us.

Wherever I have seen Hot Spots emerge on a regular basis, I have found that the executive group, often working closely with the human resource function, have engaged with the five distinct phases of activity shown in Figure 8.1.

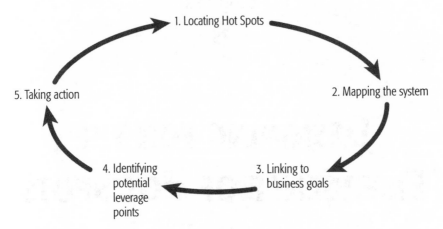

Figure 8.1 The five phases of designing for the emergence of Hot Spots

- **Phase 1: Locating Hot Spots.** These executives have a point of view about the current state of the company and where Hot Spots have already emerged. They also have a view of where Hot Spots are failing to emerge and where the country clubs and silos are located, and where the Big Freeze has taken over.

- **Phase 2: Mapping the system.** In developing this point of view about Hot Spots, these executives have an understanding of what factors have actively shaped the context in which Hot Spots emerge. They understand the norms, practices, processes, and behavior of the company and the impact these have on Hot Spots.

- **Phase 3: Linking to business goals.** Perhaps the most important aspect is that these executives have a point of view about the gap between the current emergence of Hot Spots and what is required by the goals of the business. They have found that this gap analysis is crucial to their determining where the resources and energies to craft the context of Hot Spots could be best deployed.

- **Phase 4: Identifying potential leverage points.** Most executives understand that there are many different avenues of action they can take to support the emergence of Hot Spots. This book has identified scores of possible actions. The challenge here is to recognize of all the changes that can be made the three or four that would make a real and significant difference.

- **Phase 5: Taking action.** Hot Spots emerge because people have the courage to make a difference. They have the courage to change their own behaviors and the context around them. Inevitably, when the Hot Spots and areas of Big Freeze have been diagnosed, the system has been mapped, and the extent of the gap has been established, there are a whole host of possible actions that can be taken. Executives who are successful champions of Hot Spots have the courage to establish a course of action that will significantly increase the probability of Hot Spots spontaneously arising in the future.

The sequence of these five phases is crucial. Without the rigorous diagnosis that enables us to locate Hot Spots and areas of reduced energy, we may be significantly overestimating or underestimating the extent of the energy available. Without mapping the system, we are in danger of underestimating the way in which the whole system works together and falling back on leverage points that have served us well in the past rather than exploring new ways to create fertile ground for Hot Spots to blossom. Without an understanding of where Hot Spots will be crucial in the future, we are in danger of failing to allocate scarce resources to the areas of the business that most need it; and without establishing a course of action, we are in danger of simply addressing the "low-hanging fruit" rather than addressing the bigger issues that need to be addressed.

These five phases form a natural sequence. They are not a one-off intervention but rather a repeating cycle of diagnosis and action that executives should consider engaging on an annual or biannual basis. This cycling through the five phases is crucial because Hot Spots and the energy that accompanies them can dissipate rapidly. Hot Spots are not static phenomena; they can emerge or disappear in the blink of an eye. So to understand where they are emerging and where we need them to emerge, we need to keep a close eye on the energy states within the company.

Phase 1: Locating Hot Spots

The first diagnostic phase is about putting on the metaphorical thermal goggles to identify where Hot Spots are located across the company and partnerships and where the Big Freeze has taken over.

How can this be achieved? In the Hot Spots study, my colleagues and I have developed a battery of employee surveys to establish the extent to which people are engaged in Hot Spots. We follow up our initial diagnosis with focus groups and one-on-one interviews to get a deeper understanding of what is actually happening. Many companies use employee surveys on a relatively frequent basis. In my experience, most executives have a plethora of information about the experiences and expectations of employees. What they lack is a diagnostic capacity to make sense of the information that they have. So the goal of the first phase is to use the data a company already has to locate the energy fields in the company.

Appendix A, "Resources for Creating Hot Spots," traces out the entire process and provides a range of tools to support you as you locate Hot Spots. Section A.1.1 presents a set of questions that will enable you and your colleagues to assess the extent to which the first three essential elements of a Hot Spot (a cooperative mindset, boundary spanning, and an igniting purpose) are currently in place in your team, business, function, or company. You and your colleagues can present and consider these profiles for each of these three elements in section A.1.2. The final diagnostic, in section A.1.3, provides a set of questions by which you can assess the current productive capacity of Hot Spots, the final essential element. These four scores allow you to calculate a single score that represents the probability of productive Hot Spots emerging in the parts of the organization that you and your colleagues have studied. This part of the appendix ends with further questions about the current location of Hot Spots that you can ask and discuss.

The aim here is to use this diagnosis in various parts of the company to begin to build an overall picture of the company with regard to areas of high energy and potential energy and areas of low energy, where Hot Spots are unlikely to emerge.

The important aspect of this diagnosis is that we are looking at the individual's beliefs and experiences, aggregated at the level of the group. Groups that constitute Hot Spots may not be confined to the organizational structures of the company. They may go across the boundaries of formal work groups to project teams and communities of practice. It is important to leave this first diagnostic phase with an idea of the typology of the business with regard to Hot Spots—where they seem to be emerging and where the energy levels are low due to the absence of one or more elements.

Phase 2: Mapping the System

You now have an idea of the energy typography of the company—where the energy for Hot Spots is located, where energy has been depleted, and the extent of development of the first three essential elements. You understand where the Hot Spots are but at this stage know very little about why these areas of energy have emerged or what can be done to increase the probability of their flourishing as Hot Spots. To understand why Hot Spots have emerged and why in other cases one or more elements failed to come to fruition, you need to take a closer look at the context of the emergence of Hot Spots from a systemic perspective. That is, you need to map the whole system that creates Hot Spots and identify the factors in the system that need to be strengthened. At the same time, you can map the whole system that has created the Big Freeze and identify the aspects that need to be reduced and changed.

The principles of mapping the system of emergence are as follows:

- Establish the likely points of leverage.

- Map the system of Hot Spots.

- Map the system of the Big Freeze.

Establishing the likely points of leverage

In my Hot Spot research program, my colleagues and I were able to identify the points of leverage typically (but by no means always) associated with the emergence of a Hot Spot. As a first step to mapping the system, it is useful to measure these leverage points in your own organization.

Section A.2.1 of Appendix A lets you rate some of these potential levers in your current organization or business. The rating scores for this analysis can be collated and presented in section A.2.2. It is very likely that in your own company, you have many more possible leverage points than those listed and you are encouraged in the appendix to consider what these might be.

At this stage, it is possible to consider and contrast the data from the diagnosis of the Hot Spots with the data from the diagnosis of levers. This comparison can provide important insights about why and how Hot Spots are emerging. In the appendix, you will find a series of questions to answer and discuss.

Mapping the system of Hot Spots

There are many possible combinations of barriers and leverage points to the emergence of Hot Spots. The challenge is for you and your colleagues to identify those that could make a real difference. To do this, you need to observe the emergence of a Hot Spot as the result of a complex organizational system of levers that could be practices, processes, norms, or behaviors.

The idea is to do this for all of the groups or businesses you are focusing on, in order for you and your colleagues to create a map of where the Hot Spots are located and the likely impact of the leverage points.

By way of illustration, the map presented in Figure 8.2 shows the probable leverage points for a Hot Spot that emerged in a major U.S. company. This Hot Spot was located in teams and project groups that spanned the R&D and marketing functions of the company. This Hot Spot had been enormously successful, and the people involved had created a stream of important innovations through the novel combination of the knowledge held within each function.

The map of the system shows the two key functional groups, R&D and marketing, with the Hot Spot emerging across the boundaries between them. Around the Hot Spot are the first three essential elements: a cooperative mindset, cross-boundary working, and an igniting purpose. Attached to each of these three elements are the levers that appeared to play a role in supporting the emergence of the Hot Spot. The dotted lines connecting these leverage points show the major relationships between the levers and the three elements. The direction of the arrows shows the likely direction of causality.

Note that I have identified seven leverage points that the executive team believed had made a significant impact on the emergence of the Hot Spot: the bonuses that are paid to cross-functional teams, the extensive use of communication technology, the manner in which the key roles rotate among the senior team members, the long-term focus on cultural diversity, the team leaders development program, the extensive and systematic training of managers in dialogue techniques, and the modeling of cooperative behavior by the senior leaders.

These leverage points often made a more significant impact on one of the elements. For example, the capacity of the senior leaders to model cooperative behavior was a leverage point for a cooperative mindset. In many cases, these leverage points do not simply affect a single element but rather also support and reinforce each other. An illustration of this reinforcing potential of leverage points is the investment that had been made in training in dialogue techniques for a significant proportion of the middle and senior managers of each function. As you can see in the model, these dialogue competencies had a significant and positive leverage on the cooperative mindset since part of the training increased managers' capacity to converse cooperatively with each other. It also increased the potential of managers to ask igniting question and also the capacity of the senior leaders to model cooperative behavior.

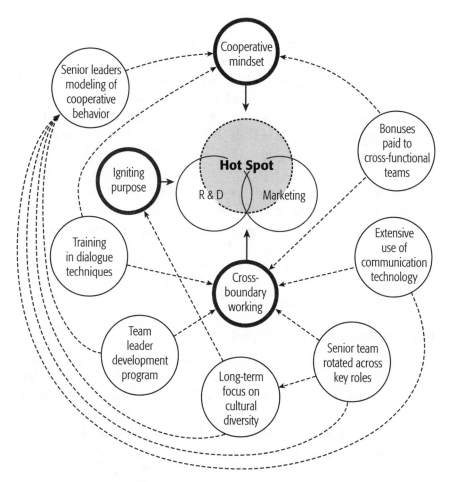

Figure 8.2 The Hot Spot scenario: mapping emergence

A glance at the model shows other important leverage points. For example, the team leader development program, a two-week cross-functional program, leveraged cross-boundary working and also influenced the formation of close cooperative working relationships between members and alumni of the program. Similarly, igniting purpose was probably leveraged by the training in dialogue that many of the senior executives had received. It was also leveraged with a long-term focus on cultural diversity within the management cadres that ensured that a proportion of members always came from emerging markets. The impact this cultural diversity had on the igniting purpose was clear. With their different perspectives, these managers were capable of asking questions others had not considered and also of bringing a unique point of view to the debates.

Section A.2.3 of Appendix A provides a simple map (the basis of our Figure 8.2) that you and your colleagues can play around with as a way of thinking about how the key points of leverage may actually affect the first three essential elements of a Hot Spot and indeed their possible relationships with each other. These models and the discussions that accompany them are important because they will draw your attention to the dynamics of the system. Thus you are reminded of and can discuss the implications of removing any current point of leverage. For example, in the model presented in Figure 8.2, removing the team leaders development program will have a potentially damaging impact on cross-boundary working and on the cooperative modeling of the senior leaders. This does not mean that you and your colleagues should consider every aspect of the model sacrosanct and unchangeable. However, it does mean that if a lever is removed, something else has to be put in its place.

Mapping the system of the Big Freeze

You and your colleagues will need to consider both where Hot Spots are emerging, and where they are not emerging. This enables you to understand more clearly what is acting as a barrier to emergence. To do this, you can follow the same sequence as mapping the Hot Spot system, as illustrated in Figure 8.3, where instead of the Hot Spot at the center we have the Big Freeze. Arrayed around it are the three elements we know will be potentially playing a part in the emergence of the Big Freeze: a competitive mindset, a silo mentality, and lost energy. (This illustration is hypothetical; I have created it to illustrate how the Hot Spot we considered earlier could become the Big Freeze.)

You might anticipate that a whole host of often unrelated organizational practices and processes can together lead to the emergence of a competitive mindset and a silo mentality between the R&D group and the other groups in the company.

Imagine that instead of the team leader development program, the senior team has decided to focus on creating a program in which people are developed in teams within each of their functions and separate businesses, rather than building a development program in which people from across businesses and functions participate. Although this will provide deep and useful knowledge, it has two potentially unintended consequences that stifle the possibility of a Hot Spot emerging. First, as a consequence of the program

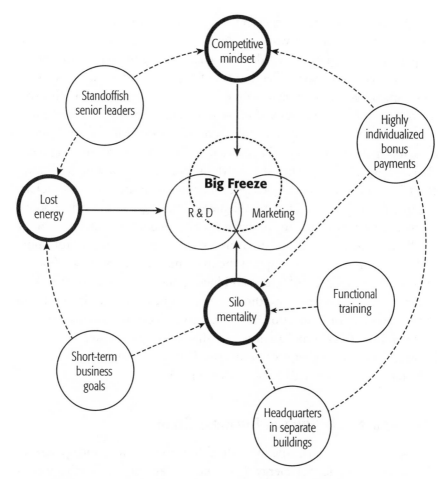

Figure 8.3 The Big Freeze scenario: blocking emergence of Hot Spots

members of each function will spend more and more time together. Over time the group norms will strengthen and the barriers between the function and other parts of the company will become ever more distinct and impermeable. Second, there will be a lack of job movement across the functions. As a consequence of development programs within functions and business, the strong group norms that have emerged have ensured that people feel much more comfortable with members of their own group and are less likely to have the courage to move or cross boundaries. This silo mentality can be subtly reinforced through other practices. For example, if the R&D headquarters and the marketing headquarters are in different cities, the respective senior teams have few opportunities to meet informally and form bonds of trust.

This potential lack of trust between the senior teams will reinforce norms of competition between the two functions. The resulting lack of a mindset of cooperation will significantly reduce the chances of ignition of a Hot Spot.

You might also imagine that instead of bonuses paid to the members of cross-functional teams, individualized bonuses are handed out. In this scenario, it is in the best interests of the senior teams to build their own group and watch over it rather than to attempt to collaborate with others. None of these factors separately would be sufficient to drain the energy from a potential Hot Spot. However, when they work together, they have a multiplicative effect. The unintended consequences of short-term business goals, headquarters in separate buildings, function-centered training, and individual bonus payments together reduce the probability of a Hot Spot emerging.

By now you have established the extent and location of Hot Spots within the business, have mapped the dynamics that appear to influence the emergence of the Hot Spots, and have gained some idea of the likely capacity of the energy within the Hot Spot to be productively employed in improvement or innovation. Before we consider how and where to take action, it is crucial to build an understanding of the gap between where the business requires the energy of productive Hot Spots and where this energy is currently emerging. This is the basis of phase 3.

Phase 3: Linking to Business Goals

Hot Spots play a crucial role in the health of the organization. Wherever Hot Spots are found, the energy they generate can make a significant contribution to performance. However, there has to be some relationship between the goals of the business and the probable emergence of Hot Spots. So before identifying levers, it is wise to establish where in the organization these levers are best deployed. Determining the extent of the gap is an art rather than a science. However, this phase can be approached by actively visualizing the future business goals and needs for knowledge and innovation translated into Hot Spots. This visualization tool is presented in section A.3.1 of Appendix A. This section also contains a set of questions that you and your colleagues can answer and discuss.

From those conversations, it will be possible for you and your colleagues to map the company with regard to where Hot Spots would be most useful to meeting the goals of the business. Let me give you an example of the sorts of issues that may arise. In one large European commercial bank, the business goals for the next five years had two primary thrusts: the expansion of the bank into Asia and the continued reduction of the cost base of the company. As senior team members visualized the expansion into Asia, they began to map where Hot Spots could play a crucial role. They saw Hot Spots emerging in three prime locations: within the initial expansion team, in the series of partnerships with local Asian banks that would fuel the expansion, and in the European and Asian functional teams charged with knowledge transfer. The probability of the business goal being met would crucially depend on the emergence of these Hot Spots. If the Big Freeze took over or the businesses became silos, energy would be depleted and the business goals would go unmet. Therefore, when the executives considered current Hot Spots, they were able to make an assessment of whether the energy would be sufficient to support the emergence of future Hot Spots or if more leverage would be needed.

Phase 4: Identifying Potential Leverage Points

By this phase, you and your colleagues will have located the Hot Spots and mapped the system that would appear to encourage their emergence. You have examined the impact of the future business goals and considered the gap between the current Hot Spots and future needs. This naturally leads to a conversation about clarifying the factors currently supporting Hot Spots and those that are acting as barriers. We now focus on these potential leverage points and consider what should remain, what should be removed, and what should be developed and invented.

At any given moment, your organization's capacity to focus resources on change is strictly limited. As we saw in Figure 8.3, there are typically many reasons why the Big Freeze has emerged. In this case we saw five levers—the pay system, the functional training, the separation of the headquarters, the short-term business goals and the behavior of senior leaders. While each of these levers is important, it is unlikely that any company would have the energy or resources to tackle all five simultaneously. Doing so would simply deplete the resources of the company and result in initiative fatigue on the part of employees. So the challenge facing you and your colleagues at this phase is to identify, out of all the possible initiatives that you can take, which ones will make the maximum difference with the minimum force applied.

Imagine for a moment that you are trying to move a large object with a lever. The trick here is to deploy the laws of physics to ensure that the object is moved with as little force as possible. Every model of the emergence of

Hot Spots is unique. It is your role to arrive at a view of what must and can be changed. Although every Hot Spot is unique, there are a number of underlying principles that can act as an important aid to this decision-making process:

There are four principles for identifying leverage points for the emergence of a Hot Spot:

- Focus on leverage points rather than outcomes.
- Review actions against all possible leverage points.
- Widen the analysis of leverage points beyond the obvious.
- Bite the bullet on big resource items.

Focusing on leverage points rather than outcomes

Maps of Hot Spots often contain leverage points that are practices and processes and other points that are outcomes. These outcomes are typically cultural and normative characteristics such as "a culture of trust" or "goodwill among the senior leaders." These are crucial aspects of the Hot Spot, and their presence needs to be acknowledged. However, they are not of themselves leverage points; they are simply the outcomes of practices and processes. For example, it is not possible to put resources directly into developing "a culture of trust" by changing the value statements of the company to emphasize trust. To create a culture of trust, the points of leverage are the practices, processes, routines, and habits that enable and reinforce the emergence of a culture of trust. These might include the induction practices, the way layoffs are handled, and the way in which managers are trained to interact with their team members. So if "a culture of trust" is indeed important, effort must be focused on understanding the leverage points that act as enablers or barriers. Simply focusing on the outcomes will have little impact and will be interpreted as rhetoric rather than action.

Reviewing actions against all possible leverage points

In this phase, you and your colleagues are considering ways of changing practices, processes, routines, and habits to improve the probability of Hot Spots emerging. Identifying leverage points for change is not easy. It requires looking at unexamined practices and assumptions about how work is done and how people connect with each other. The first step is to think expansively about how changing practices and processes would help create the elements of a Hot Spot. The purpose is to brainstorm and, for the moment, not let questions about feasibility overwhelm the discussion. Thinking out of the box about leverage points is difficult because we tend to accept that there is no other way of doing things.

In brainstorming possible leverage points, it is wise to take a brief look at the whole portfolio of possible levers. This initial brainstorm reveals an array of potential leverage points. However, my experience is that at times like this, we tend to return to the actions we are most familiar and comfortable with. To get the widest array of potential leverage points, it is useful during this step to actively seek to expand the analysis of potential leverage points beyond the obvious. A way of thinking about this is presented in section A.4.1 of Appendix A.

Widening the analysis of potential leverage points beyond the obvious

Use of the potential leverage points depends on the extent to which current investment and resources have been allocated to them and their relative ease of implementation.

Levers with significant current investment, which are relatively easy to implement, tend to be the habitual levers that are pulled whenever change is deemed to be important. I saw this in a large manufacturing company. For over a decade, successive executive teams had put enormous emphasis on and resources into management training. For numerous historical reasons, training was regarded as a significant lever for change. This was a major financial commitment, but it was also relatively easy for the executives to implement. In the previous decade, the executive team had agreed to a portfolio of training programs and made a significant financial investment in the company's training center. As a consequence, whenever the executives faced a challenge concerning behavior, they naturally turned to the highly competent and well-resourced training function to design a training intervention that would meet their needs.

When we met with the executives to talk about Hot Spots emerging in a particularly important part of the company, their natural bias was to return to their habitual response and to continue investing in training. A consequence of the historical commitment to training was an overemphasis on training as a solution to every challenge they faced. Investment in training had become a knee-jerk response and over time had straitjacketed their

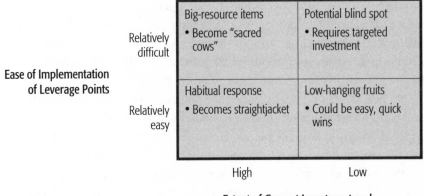

	High	Low
Relatively difficult	Big-resource items • Become "sacred cows"	Potential blind spot • Requires targeted investment
Relatively easy	Habitual response • Becomes straightjacket	Low-hanging fruits • Could be easy, quick wins

Ease of Implementation of Leverage Points

Extent of Current Investment and
Resource Allocation to Leverage Points

Figure 8.4 Widening the analysis of potential leverage points beyond the obvious

actions. The challenge for this executive team was to build a greater aware-ness of other leverage points that were relatively easy to implement but for which there had been limited investment—in other words, to identify their "blind spots." For example, although there had been much investment in functional training, there had been very little investment in cross-functional training. Simply making some of the training events cross-functional was relatively easy and had the potential to make an important contribution to the emergence of Hot Spots by supporting cross-boundary cooperation.

In this case, the executives were moving horizontally across the matrix in Figure 8.4. They had transformed a leverage point (functional training) of high current investment to one that they had not currently invested in (cross-functional training). Since they remained within the historical lever-age points, the transformation was relatively easy for them to implement.

Biting the bullet on big-resource items

There are times when widening the analysis of leverage points beyond the obvious begins to include leverage points that will be more difficult to implement. In a major investment bank, I found that enormous resources had gone into coaching members of the senior team. Each executive mem-ber had a coach with whom he or she met on a regular basis. The executives originally resisted the idea of executive coaching, considering it intrusive and unnecessary. It was only through the intervention of a trusted adviser that the executive team had been persuaded down this route. This was certainly a "big-resource item," both in terms of resources expended and commitments required. However, over time, what had started as an important leverage point became something of a sacred cow. So much emotional energy had been expended on implementation and gaining executive commitment that it became difficult to question whether using the leverage point of the individual executive coaches was indeed the right answer.

This question came to the fore when the executive team mapped the current impact of the levers on the likely emergence of Hot Spots. When the executives analyzed the model, they discovered that the resources focused on coaching had indeed had a positive impact on the executives' behavior and their capacity to serve as positive role models for others. However, it had little impact on the cross-boundary working that would be so crucial going forward. In fact, there was some evidence that the individual coaching had actually isolated the executive team members from each other as they focused more and more energy on their relationship with their coach, to the detriment of their relationships with each other. This difficult-to-implement leverage point had become a sacred cow. As the team members pondered the Hot Spot element of cross-boundary working, they began to understand that what would be crucial as a leverage point going forward would be team-based rather than individual coaching. To expand the analysis beyond the sacred cows requires an executive team that is willing and able to question investment decisions, even when important commitments have been made to these leverage points in the past.

Eventually, it is crucial to bite the bullet and focus on leverage points that are difficult to implement and not areas of current investment. In my analysis of Hot Spot leverage points, I have found that rewards often fall into this category. By way of illustration, in one company I studied, a highly individualized bonus system was having a strong negative impact on the cross-boundary element of the Hot Spot. Although people cooperated within their groups, there was no incentive for them to cooperate across boundaries, and in fact the bonus scheme was a strong disincentive. The individualized bonus scheme had become something of a sacred cow; it had been championed and supported by a senior sales executive who believed it played a crucial role in pushing the performance of the teams. Attempts at tampering with the bonus scheme were met with strong resistance.

Concentrating on leverage points where there is already a strong commitment to investment and ease of implementation will have the effect of important easy wins. However, you need to look beyond these easy wins.

It is often the hard-to-implement leverage points, like team-based rewards, that become blind spots. These blind spots are typically areas where investment has been minimal and where implementing change is seen as difficult. However, there are occasions when "blind spot" leverage points that have been disregarded in the past can make a real and significant contribution to performance improvements and increased innovative capacity. To capitalize on these, executive teams have to be thoughtful about the fifth phase, taking action.

◘ Phase 5: Taking Action

Through the first four phases, you have established where Hot Spots are currently blazing and where the Big Freeze is emerging. Modeling the leverage points has allowed you to create a shared view of potential leverage points that could be supported in the future, and expanding the analysis creates a broader and potentially more creative view of potentially significant leverage points. Now is the time to move into action. Leverage points that have had high investment in the past and those that can be implemented with ease do not require any specific attention. Leverage points that are difficult to implement or will require significant resource investment call for a more nuanced and more sophisticated approach. As in the earlier phases, each team finds its own way of achieving this. There are a few broad principles that can play an important role in ensuring that actions are taken to maximize the potential for productive Hot Spots to emerge in locations and at times when they are most needed:

- Make the business case.
- Use experiments to calibrate the benefits.
- Work with the forces for and against change.

Making the business case

It is relatively easy to implement leverage points that have a history of successful use. It is also relatively easy to implement leverage points for which there is current executive support. However, as you saw in Figure 8.4 , not all leverage points fall into these categories. Some will be difficult to implement and are not current sources of investment allocation.

It is possible to build leverage points that are currently blind spots. To do so requires making a strong business case for investment.

Using experiments to calibrate the benefits

Earlier you saw how the executive team at the U.K. telecom company BT laid the groundwork for ignition around the idea of how to increase customer satisfaction. The company has a long history of innovative practices and processes. For example, in 1990, employee engagement data from the engineering group at BT showed that this was becoming an increasingly disengaged and disheartened group. The Big Freeze had taken over. The engineers were unwilling to work cooperatively with each other. When the members of the executive team examined the situation, they realized that the stress the engineers felt was driving a mindset of competition rather then cooperation. They felt so overwhelmed by the pressure of their work that they were working more and more as individuals and less and less cooperatively. The executive team began to realize that moving toward a cooperative mindset would require fundamentally changing the way the engineers worked.

The idea was initially met coolly by both managers and engineers. This was definitely a blind spot, an area of low current investment where change was perceived to be relatively difficult to implement. In the past, BT had made little use of work redesign, the capacity to redesign work was poorly developed, and the preferred habitual response was to roll out short-term reengaging programs. However, a couple of members of the executive team agreed to champion job redesign and began to build the business case through a series of experiments.

They began by designing three experimental conditions. In the first condition, nothing was changed about the way in which the engineers worked. In the second condition, they used the favored, habitual response and ran a two-day reengagement program. In the third condition, the executive team set about working with the engineers to redesign the way in which work was done with the view to reducing time pressure and stress.

The thinking behind the three experiments began by *defining the evaluation criteria*. What business measures should be used to evaluate success? The executives chose three: absence rates (the number of days per month the engineers took sick leave), engagement of the engineers with their work (using a survey with twenty engagement items), and measures of productivity, particularly the cooperation of team members and the team rate of productivity. This initial evaluation step is critical; otherwise, it is impossible to evaluate the extent of change across the subsequent period of experimentation.

The executive team and a group of engineers then went about *considering what they could do in the three experimental conditions.* For the first group of engineers, nothing was done. In the second group of engineers, a one-week reengagement program was developed. For the third, a design team was created to determine the best way to come up with a work design that would support cooperative working. The team quickly determined that the key was to design more flexibility and choice into where and when the engineers worked. Of course, this was not straightforward. Some kinks had to be ironed out, and some aspects of the intervention ran into various obstacles. Redesigning the work of the engineer was by definition violating some basic assumptions and taken-for-granted norms. In this case, the work of the engineering team had been closely supervised by a group of managers whose role was to create the worksheets for the engineers and keep an eye on their productivity. Building in flexibility and individual schedules made the job of the managers more complex and also resulted in their losing much of the control they had previously enjoyed. So the experiment around job redesign required the engineering group to suspend, if only temporarily, some of the operating procedures that were identified as barriers to flexible working.

Over time, the engineers in the third experimental condition, who were working more flexibly, made extensive use of technology that enabled them to work from home for part of the workweek. The design team also worked closely with the engineers to redesign their schedules so that they had more choice to work at certain times. This flexibility took much of the pressure off engineers and gave them more time to work cooperatively with their colleagues and to share the tacit knowledge and insights that let them carry out their jobs more quickly and more accurately.

After one year, the senior team took stock of the evaluating criteria: absence rates, employee engagement, and productivity in each of the three conditions. In the first condition, there was no change. In the second, there was a slight initial change, but after six months, the rates fell back to normal. In the third condition, the engineering team was on average 20 percent more productive and 20 percent more engaged, and absence rates had decreased significantly. This evaluation step is crucial. All experiments are fragile, and without tangible benefits to employees and the visible support of key decision makers, they are likely to be only transitory.

By participating in this well-designed series of experiments, the executives were able to build a strong business case for job redesign, which had previously been considered difficult to implement and toward which limited resources had been directed. As a result of this experiment, over the subsequent five-year period, significant investment was made in job rede-sign and in efforts to create a context within which Hot Spots were more likely to emerge. A set of questions around experimentation are presented in section A.5.1 of Appendix A.

Working with the forces for and against change

Building a clear business case for action and using experimentation to iden-tify the likely extent of the actions taken is crucial. Sometimes this is not sufficient. This is particularly the case when the situations that have created the Big Freeze are strongly embedded within the organization and seen as "the way we do business around here." Take, for example, the situation in a major multinational electronics firm. The initial assessment of Hot Spots showed that very limited innovation was taking place in the company's main Asian market. Analysis of the first three essential elements suggested that what was missing was cross-boundary working, particularly between headquarters and the Asian groups. A more detailed analysis suggested that a major trigger for this was the lack of Asian nationals at the senior execu-tive level in the organization. It seemed obvious that what was needed to support cross-boundary working was more Asians on the senior team. Yet even though many members of the senior team acknowledged this, nothing had been done to make use of this potential leverage point.

To understand why requires us to move beyond a simple rational description of the leverage points to a deeper understanding of the forces that are working to support these levers and those forces that are working against it. This simple tool is based on the concept of force field analysis. Simply put, in every desired end state (add more Asian executives), there are forces that are currently operating for the end state and forces that are currently operating against it. These forces for and against change are bal-anced; as a consequence, working only on forces for change significantly increases the forces against change. To move into action, executives have to work on increasing the driving forces while reducing the restraining forces. To do this, they have to first debate and agree on a list of the forces operating both for and against change. A summary of this is presented in Table 8.1.

The force field analysis suggests that action has to take place in increasing and reinforcing the brand in Asia and promoting the idea of an employer of choice, in making greater use of acquisitions as a source of talent, and in working on reducing turnover rates through a renewed emphasis on mentoring and induction.

Table 8.1 Force field analysis on crossing boundaries

Question: What forces in the company are driving and restraining the recruitment and retention of Asian executives?	
Driving forces	**Restraining forces**
The recruitment of Asian executives is widely accepted as a crucial lever for change.	Corporate culture is very headquarters-orientated, with other countries seen as "outposts."
Competitors are actively recruiting and retaining Asian executives.	Career planning occurs within rather than across companies.
The steady growth of the brand in Asia is attracting higher-potential executives.	A number of high-profile Asian recruits have left within a year of joining.
Company is beginning to be seen as an employer of choice for Chinese graduates.	Turnover rates of graduates in India and China have been high.
Acquisitions and joint ventures have created a pool of senior talent in Asia.	"Old boys' club" at headquarters makes it difficult for new executives to join.
Networks and exchange programs have built the brand with younger people.	Current human resource systems are poor at supporting multinational recruitment.

Conclusion

In designing for the emergence of Hot Spots, the five phases of locating, mapping, linking, identifying levers, and taking action create a sequence of actions that together increase the probability of Hot Spots emerging.

Hot Spots arise spontaneously, yet there is much we can do to support and encourage their emergence. As individuals, we owe it to ourselves to seek out and become members of Hot Spots, and the companies for whom we work have a duty to lay the groundwork for and leverage Hot Spots. There is much we can do—we just need courage and determination to create a universe of Hot Spots.

CHAPTER SUMMARY

DESIGNING FOR THE EMERGENCE OF HOT SPOTS

Key Points

Hot Spots are emergent phenomena; they cannot be summoned forth or controlled. Their development requires a move from the old rules of domination to the new rules of emergence, under which relationships, purposeful conversation, and boundary spanning are crucial and the emphasis is on ignition of latent energy supported by unique signature processes. Fundamentally, Hot Spots are events during which value is created by exploiting what is currently known and exploring what is currently unknown.

There are five phases of activities that executives must engage in to create an environment in which Hot Spots can emerge:

- Profile the current terrain of energy in order to identify places where Hot Spots are naturally occurring and those where the Big Freeze is predominant.

- Map the system that supports the emergence of the current Hot Spots and Big Freezes in order to establish the likely system of causality and the key practices, processes, norms, and behaviors.

- Link the business goals—both short-term and longer-term—to Hot Spot requirements. Where in the company is it crucial for Hot Spots to emerge? The gap between current Hot Spots and future needs establishes the extent to which change is required.

- Identify the potential leverage points that need to be enhanced for Hot Spots to emerge, and be sure to consider leverage points that are less than obvious.

- Take action on these potential leverage points, using experimentation to make the business case, and taking due regard of the forces operating for and against change.

A

RESOURCES FOR
CREATING HOT SPOTS

THERE ARE MANY ACTIONS we can take as individuals to lay the groundwork for the emergence of Hot Spots. We can think about our cooperative behavior and decide to work more cooperatively with others. We can become more aware of the positive impact working across boundaries can have and perhaps develop our own boundary spanning capability. And of course, we can harness our courage to ask inspiring questions and develop inspiring tasks. Hot Spots are made up of people, so it makes sense that personal action can increase the probability of their emerging. But Hot Spots are more than just individuals; they are also about the relationships between individuals and the communities in which they work. Hot Spots emerge as a consequence of an interrelated system of practices and processes; behaviors and competencies. This appendix addresses this interrelated system through a number of diagnostics, profiling tools, mapping techniques, and questions. These tools and techniques follow the phases described in Chapter 8.

This appendix begins, in the first phase, with a diagnosis and mapping technique designed to help you and your colleagues consider the *current location of Hot Spots* throughout your business. Once you have created a view of the current location of Hot Spots, you can move on to the second phase, which presents a series of diagnostic and mapping techniques that enable you to consider how and why these Hot Spots emerged. The emphasis here is to develop deeper clarity by *mapping the system.* This involves identifying "levers" that could potentially be part of the system of emergence and then modeling these levers and the relationships between them and the four essential elements of a Hot Spot. In the third phase, there is a visualization tool and a series of questions to support you as you consider the future needs of the business and therefore where the emergence of Hot Spots would be most advantageous. By this time, you and your colleagues will have an overview of the *extent of the gap* between where you are now with regard to Hot Spots and where the business needs the energy and innovative capacity of Hot Spots in the future. Reducing the gap and supporting the emergence of Hot Spots for the future will require clarity about what needs to change through the *identification of potential leverage points.* To do this successfully may well require that you and your colleagues come to terms with any blind spots and reconsider where your resources can be best targeted. Once you are clear about what needs to change, my advice is to begin *experimentation* to identify the contextual issues and calibrate the possible benefits and unintended consequences.

A word about how to proceed. It is possible to progress through these resources as an individual. In fact, that is a useful way to start. But as you now realize, Hot Spots arise as a result of a whole system, rarely from the endeavors of a single individual. So once you are familiar with this appendix, it would be useful to engage a team in a series of Hot Spot conversations. In the spirit of Hot Spots, of course, my advice would be to ensure that the membership of these teams spans boundaries. It is a wonderful opportunity for people from human resources, marketing, and finance together with the business streams to think really hard about Hot Spots. The tools and diagnostics, models, and steps are designed to be resources. You don't have to progress through every phase, although there is a natural order, and you don't have to engage in every question, although they may all turn out to be useful.

So take a look at this appendix, persuade an interesting group of people to share a conversation with you, and set aside half a day for a trial run. You may be amazed at what you find—and amazed at how simple it can be. With just a few well-chosen interventions, you and your colleagues may be preparing to make a significant contribution to Hot Spots and therefore to the long-term health of your company.

Two appendixes follow this one. Appendix B provides an overview of the literature on Hot Spots, and Appendix C gives an overview of the methodology my colleagues and I used in our research, to provide greater insight into how we designed out studies and the models we tested.

May your world be ablaze with Hot Spots!

Phase 1: Locating Hot Spots

Hot Spots are idiosyncratic to each company and time. Therefore, the initial phase is to build a deep and profound understanding of the current state of the company. You need to understand precisely where Hot Spots have already emerged. You also need to establish where Hot Spots are failing to emerge. There may be places that are essentially "country clubs"—where cooperation may be high, but there is no real igniting purpose and therefore limited focus and energy around a goal. There may be places that are essentially "silos"— where groups, functions or businesses have erected barriers around themselves and where cross-boundary cooperation is low. There may indeed be places where the Big Freeze has taken over, with little cooperation and goodwill.

A.1.1 Diagnosis of the first three essential elements of Hot Spots

The following diagnosis is designed to enable you to establish the extent to which the elements of a Hot Spot are currently in place in a group, a community, a business, or a company. You may want to distribute this diagnosis to people and groups around the company and then collate the responses.

Consider each statement, and assign a rating from 1 to 5, using the following scale: 1 (strongly disagree), 2 (disagree), 3 (neither agree nor disagree), 4 (agree), 5 (strongly agree).

Item 1	I really trust the people I work with.	1	2	3	4	5
Item 2	There is a feeling of give-and-take in the group.	1	2	3	4	5
Item 3	Here people cooperate willingly with each other.	1	2	3	4	5
Item 4	People from outside the group very often share their knowledge and insights with people within my group.	1	2	3	4	5
Item 5	People from outside the group are very positive and enthusiastic about working with me and my colleagues.	1	2	3	4	5

(*Continues on page 176*)

Item 6	There are many occasions when I work in project teams or task forces with people outside of my group.	1	2	3	4	5
Item 7	I feel excited about and engaged with the work I do.	1	2	3	4	5
Item 8	The tasks I do are meaningful and resonate with my own values.	1	2	3	4	5
Item 9	I feel that the work I do is aligned with the vision of the business.	1	2	3	4	5

Total Cooperative Mindset Score (Item 1, Item 2, Item 3) =
Total Boundary Spanning Score (Item 4, Item 5, Item 6) =
Total Igniting Purpose Score (Item 7, Item 8, Item 9) =

Now plot the separate scores on the graph in section A.1.2.

A.1.2 Mapping the first three elements

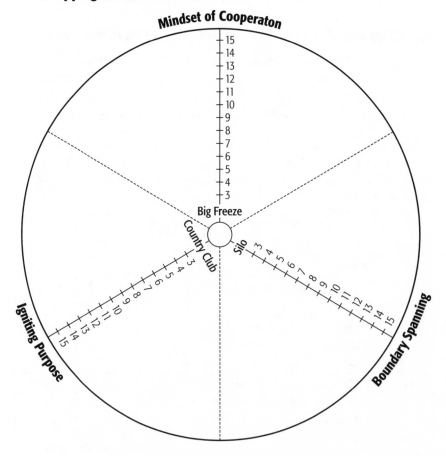

A.1.3 Diagnosing the productive capacity of Hot Spots

The following exercise is designed to enable you to establish the extent of the productive capacity in groups, communities, a business, or your company.

Consider each statement, and assign a rating from 1 to 5, using the following scale: 1 (strongly disagree), 2 (disagree), 3 (neither agree nor disagree), 4 (agree), 5 (strongly agree).

Item 1	We use technology in a way that creates a feeling of intimacy with people who are distant.	1	2	3	4	5
Item 2	We have a number of practices that encourage people to share information about each other and build a shared sense of their competencies and preferences.	1	2	3	4	5
Item 3	We have created a wide degree of flexibility that enables people to work at their own pace and yet with sufficient integration that their efforts can be pulled together.	1	2	3	4	5
Item 4	We use a great deal of feedback about progress so that people can coordinate their activities.	1	2	3	4	5
Item 5	We use conflict resolution practices that encourage issues to be surfaced and then worked through.	1	2	3	4	5
Item 6	We experience periods of time pressure interspersed with times for reflection and purposeful conversation.	1	2	3	4	5

Total Productive Capacity Score =
   (Divide total score by 2) =

Calculate Hot Spot Probability:
   [(Cooperative Mindset × Boundary Spanning × Igniting Purpose) × Productive Capacity] ÷ 100

Example: $[(11 \times 6 \times 7) \times 5] = 2,310 \div 100 = 23.1$

Scoring: 0–99 Low probability of productive Hot Spots emerging
   100–199 Some probability of productive Hot Spots emerging
   200–500 High probability of productive Hot Spots emerging

Phase 1 questions: assessing your profile of Hot Spots

Hot Spots are crucial to organizational health and prosperity; these questions help you and your colleagues think about your Hot Spot profile.

1. In what parts of the company do you believe Hot Spots are occurring? Are there any surprises here? Places you thought might have high probability but don't? Places where you are pleasantly surprised?

2. Where Hot Spots have failed to emerge and the Big Freeze prevails, what do you believe to be some of the barriers?

3. Take a closer look at one area where you believe a Hot Spot has emerged. What are the main drivers and points of leverage for the emergence of the Hot Spot? What do you think really made a difference?

4. In what parts of the company do you believe the Big Freeze has settled in? Are there any surprises here? What do you think has really made a difference?

5. Are there any trends emerging with regard to cooperative mindset, boundary spanning, or igniting purpose?

6. Is there more you could be doing to diagnose the emergence of a Hot Spot? For example, are you collecting sufficient data on a regular basis to identify Hot Spots or the Big Freeze?

Phase 2: Mapping the System

Hot Spots emerge spontaneously; they are naturally occurring phenomena. If you want to know more about the Hot Spots in your company and why they have emerged, you need to map the system of their emergence.

A.2.1 Possible leverage points for emergence of a Hot Spot

The following exercise is designed to enable you to establish the extent of some of the leverage points in your organization.

Consider each statement, and assign a rating from 1 to 5, using the following scale: 1 (strongly disagree), 2 (disagree), 3 (neither agree nor disagree), 4 (agree), 5 (strongly agree).

A Mindset of Cooperation

Item 1	The recruitment and hiring practices shield the company from overly competitive people and encourage the selection of cooperative people.	1	2	3	4	5
Item 2	The induction and socializing practices encourage people to develop cooperative working relationships.	1	2	3	4	5
Item 3	The reward practices reinforce and encourage team rather than highly individual behavior.	1	2	3	4	5
Item 4	The behavior of leaders encourages and models cooperative working.	1	2	3	4	5
Item 5	Individuals and groups are provided with facilitation, mentoring, and coaching.	1	2	3	4	5
Item 6	We take our social responsibility seriously and engage in activities that encourage people to feel part of a wider community.	1	2	3	4	5

Spanning Boundaries

Item 7	Our socialization practices ensure that from an early stage people learn as much as possible about each other's skills, competencies and work preferences.	1	2	3	4	5
Item 8	We use social events and other occasions as forums where people can express themselves and learn more about each other.	1	2	3	4	5

(*Continues on page 180*)

Item 9	People who are able to work across the boundaries of groups and businesses and to build networks between them are valued and encouraged.	1	2	3	4	5
Item 10	The behavior of our leaders and the fairness of our practices and processes create a feeling of trust and reciprocity.	1	2	3	4	5
Item 11	We make extensive use of technology that enables us to work closely with others, even across distances.	1	2	3	4	5
Item 12	We support people moving across boundaries as part of their career development.	1	2	3	4	5

An Igniting Purpose

Item 13	We develop the skills of dialogue and conversational practices that allow us to ask important igniting questions.	1	2	3	4	5
Item 14	The way we work emphasizes creating space and time for reflection and conversation.	1	2	3	4	5
Item 15	Our practices and processes enable us to select and develop senior executives who are capable of visualizing a purpose.	1	2	3	4	5

Total Cooperative Mindset Leverage Score:
    (add Items 1 through 6 and divide by 2) =

Total Boundary Spanning Leverage Score:
    (add Items 7 through 12 and divide by 2) =

Total Igniting Purpose Leverage Score
    (add Items 13 through 15) =

A.2.2 Diagnosing Hot Spots and mapping points of leverage

Now plot the current diagnosis of the leverage points in section A.2.1 directly over the results of the current extent of the location of Hot Spots you plotted in section A.1.2. Then answer the following questions about the resulting profile:

1. What are the differences between the two profiles? Looking at the current diagnosis of the leverage points, consider where you as a company are strong and where the possible leverage points are weak and underdeveloped. What impact does this have on the probable emergence of a Hot Spot?

2. What does this mean for your company and Hot Spots?

3. What other levers do you believe could be particularly important for you in the future?

A.2.3 Creating a map of the system

To this point, you have considered the levers separately. Now it is time to consider the various levers in relation to each other. Return to section A.2.1, and consider the levers that are making a difference to the first three essential elements. You might also like to consider levers that go beyond those profiled. Taking each lever in turn, consider to what extent that lever influences any one of the three elements (cooperative mindset, boundary spanning, and igniting purpose). Identify each of the key levers in a circle, and draw an arrow to show the direction of impact. When all the relationships between the levers and the three elements have been shown, consider the relationships between the levers. The map on the following page can be used as a template.

When you are finished, answer the following questions about the map of the system:

1. What are the key relationships between the levers and the three elements?

2. What are the key relationships among the levers? Are there any unintended consequences?

3. Are there reinforcing relationships that serve to support the emergence of Hot Spots?

Phase 2 questions: mapping the system

1. Looking at the key levers that are operating right now, which levers are well developed and which are underdeveloped?

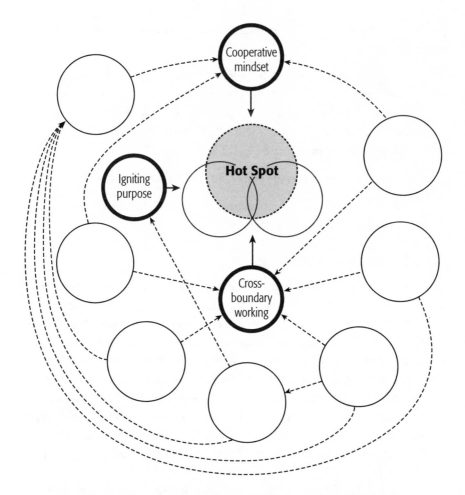

2. Are there levers that you believe are playing an important part but are not appearing on these lists? What levers are those?

3. How did the levers you identified develop? Are any of them signature processes that are unique to your company and difficult for your competitors to imitate?

4. Based on your map of the system, what are the major relationships between the various levers? Are any of them reinforcing and supporting more than one element?

5. Have you had any surprises or unexpected insights from this map?

◉ Phase 3: Linking to Business Goals

Executives have a point of view about the gap between the current emergence of Hot Spots and what is required by the goals of the business. Analysis of this gap is crucial to their determining where the resources and energies to craft the context of Hot Spots could be best deployed.

A.3.1 Visualizing the future

Visualization can be really useful here. It can take a number of forms. Begin by asking a number of your colleagues to think about the future of the business—you will need to set aside about two hours for this conversation.

Kick things off by saying:

It is ten years from now, and the company has met its major business goals. Describe how you imagine the company will be with regard to the following factors:

In what parts of the business do you believe the key source of value creation will come from the exploitation of current knowledge? *That is, in what parts of the company do you imagine that the broad product and process portfolio will remain essentially the same and productivity improvements will come from efficiency and productivity?*

In what parts of the company do you believe the key source of value creation will come from the exploration of new knowledge? That is, in what parts of the company do you imagine the broad product and process portfolio will change through radical innovation?

On a chart or chalkboard, record the responses to both questions, under the headings "Exploitation of Current Knowledge" and "Exploration of New Knowledge."

Phase 3 questions: linking to business goals

1. First take a look at the places where you are expecting to exploit the knowledge you already have.

   a. How can you retain this knowledge?

   b. What are you doing to keep people focused on these issues?

   c. How are you rewarding and supporting people to stay in these roles?

2. Now take a look at the places where you are expecting innovation to emerge—that is, where you would like to see Hot Spots.

   a. Are these the same places where you have already identified a high probability of Hot Spots?

   b. If not, what resources can you focus on these areas to increase the probability?

   c. What are the current barriers to the emergence of Hot Spots here?

⦿ Phase 4: Identifying Potential Leverage Points

Typically, construction of the model and analysis of the extent of the gap between the current and future Hot Spots are extremely interesting. The model reveals a whole host of practices, processes, norms, and other factors that appear to have an influence—both intended and unintended—on the emergence of Hot Spots. The challenge in this phase is to begin to identify and understand these potential leverage points to ensure the health of the current Hot Spots and to increase the probability of Hot Spots emerging in areas of key business needs.

A.4.1 Brainstorming potential levers

With your colleagues, spend a couple of hours thinking through this challenge. Consider the leverage points that are available to you that will increase the probability of a Hot Spot emerging. Be open to ideas and possibilities, and do not close down new avenues of thought. When considering each of these possible points of leverage, you may want to consider the following:

- **Leaders.** How might leaders' behaviors or expectations positively influence the emergence of a Hot Spot?

- **Structure.** How might the structure of the company be realigned in order to support the first three essential elements?

- **Practices and processes.** What practices and processes might encourage the emergence of a cooperative mindset, boundary spanning, igniting purpose, and productive capability?

- **Competencies and aspirations.** What skills and aspirations might support the emergence of the four elements?

A.4.2 Widening the analysis of potential leverage points beyond the obvious

It is useful here to reconsider the points of leverage you identified in section A.2.1. Taking them one by one, consider their ease of implementation and the extent of the current investment and resource allocation. Position them on the following diagram. Then consider the possible leverage points for the future. Again, think about each of these with regard to the ease of implementation and the extent of current investment. Position them also on the diagram.

	High	Low
Relatively difficult	Big-resource items • Become "sacred cows"	Potential blind spot • Requires targeted investment
Relatively easy	Habitual response • Becomes straightjacket	Low-hanging fruits • Could be easy, quick wins

Ease of Implementation of Leverage Points

Extent of Current Investment and Resource Allocation to Leverage Points

Phase 4 questions: identifying potential leverage points

1. What key points of leverage do you and your colleagues believe you should be developing for the future?

2. How many of them are potential blind spots—practices or processes you have not invested in in the past? How might you focus your attention on these areas?

3. Think hard about habitual responses: are these points of leverage that may have outlived their usefulness?

4. How do you think people will respond if you decided to invest in different practices and processes? What might be some of the forces operating for change—and what might be the forces operating against change?

Phase 5: Taking Action

Once the Hot Spots and areas of Big Freeze have been diagnosed, the system has been mapped, and the extent of the gap has been established, there are a whole host of possible actions that can be taken. The focus of this fifth phase is to establish a course of action that will significantly increase the probability of Hot Spots arising spontaneously in the future in areas of strategic business interest.

One way to think about this is to choose a couple of areas where you believe an experiment or pilot would be useful. First choose the site; then, with your colleagues, explore the following questions.

1. Define the evaluation criteria. What are the three key outcomes you will measure the experiment against?

2. Describe the experimental conditions. What are the three experimental conditions you can establish that would allow you to build a greater understanding of how to create a Hot Spot?

Phase 5 questions: taking action

1. Where in the company would you most like to see Hot Spots arise? Where are they already present? Is there a Big Freeze, a silo mentality, or a country club anywhere?

2. What are the levers you think are going to be crucial to increasing the probability of Hot Spots emerging? Are any of these blind spots?

3. What do you believe to be the major forces for and against change? How will you face these?

4. Are you prepared to run experiments and pilots? If not, why not?

5. What actions do you and your colleagues have to take now to increase the probability of High Spots emerging?

6. What behaviors do you personally have to change?

7. What skills and competencies do you personally have to develop?

B

BACKGROUND TO THE RESEARCH ON HOT SPOTS

ALTHOUGH THE CASE STUDIES and the Cooperative Advantage Research helped us describe the phenomenon of Hot Spots, they did not provide a great deal of insight about why Hot Spots actually arise. To gain a clearer understanding of the phenomenon, we spent two years immersing ourselves in the research and literature that had already been produced regarding cooperation, networks, and purpose.

The conceptual underpinnings of Hot Spots lie at the intersection of six disciplines, each with its own framing, theories, and language. Synthesizing these aspects of the six disciplines became a crucial part of the thinking for this book.

Psychology

One of the cornerstone disciplines in understanding why people choose to cooperate (or withdraw their cooperation) is the field of psychology, which provides great insight into individual behaviors, attitudes, and motivations. Psychologists, of which I am one, have a pretty clear idea about individual motivations with respect to cooperation, much of it deriving from extensive research into individual motivation conducted in the 1950s and 1960s. For Abraham Maslow, cooperation could be understood as an aspect of

what he termed the "affiliation" motivation. Simply put, people cooperate because they like to belong to something.[1] By the 1960s, psychologists
such as Richard Hackman at Harvard Business School were building a deep
understanding of group behavior and processes and how successful groups
function.[2] More recently, psychologists have focused their attention on the
microbehaviors in cooperation. In experimental laboratory studies, they
have looked at the means by which people negotiate in a group setting.
They have also brought some fascinating insights into the aspect of time
in groups and into identity and the impact of boundaries on perceptions
of in-groups and out-groups. Although there are competing psychological
theories as to why people would be motivated to cooperate, the body of
work provides some real insights.

Sociology

Over the past decade, an enormous amount of crucial research has been
conducted by sociologists into the relationships between people. A major
impetus was the groundbreaking research of Richard Putnam into the
capacity of communities to create value. His seminal work on the cities of
Italy asked why the northern cities had prospered while the southern cities
had decayed. His research showed that the northern cities were based on
wide, horizontal networks of trust and reciprocity. In contrast, the southern
cities were in the vice grip of authoritarian hierarchies that squeezed out
individual initiative and created distrust between citizens. He pointed to the
profound impact trust and what he called "reciprocity" could have on the
well-being of the citizenry and on the commercial viability of the communities.[3] The developing notion of social capital has profoundly influenced
our thinking on cooperation and is one of the key aspects of Hot Spots.

More recently, sociologists have concerned themselves with understanding the extent and value created by the networks of so-called strong
ties and weak ties between people. To do this, they have developed highly
sophisticated techniques for measuring the extent and depth of relationships
between people.[4] With regard to Hot Spots, perhaps one of the most important insights from this body of work has been the realization that under some
circumstances, greater value is created when network ties extend across functions, businesses, and organizations. The research of sociologists Ron Burt
and Mark Granovetter has profoundly influenced our understanding of how
and where value is created in networks.[5] With regard to Hot Spots, it has
brought home the difficulty but potential value created when Hot Spots bring
together diverse people who are located in different places.

Economics

Although sociology and psychology have been for me the cornerstones of thinking about Hot Spots, there is also a vast body of theory in economics about cooperation. As in other disciplines, there is no unifying theory of cooperation in economics; nevertheless, there are some strong points of view. Fundamentally, economists ask why people cooperate with others. For many economists, the overriding human motivation is self-interest. Therefore, cooperation and collaboration are described in terms of the opportunity each individual has to further his or her self-interest. The role of the institution, therefore, is to create contractual arrangements to ensure that the self-interest of the more powerful does not overwhelm that of the less powerful. As a consequence, in the field of economics, a great deal of research is devoted to "game theory," which attempts to explain how individual self-interest operates,[6] and "transaction theory," which shows how the gains from collaboration are distributed.

Historically, most theories of economics have built upward from self-interest as the defining human motivation. Over the past decade, economists such as the Nobel Prize winner Amartya Sen have brought into play other motivational concepts such as altruism.[7] Their voice has added weight to a growing debate in economics about the meaning of cooperation and collaboration. In particular, there has been a rigorous debate between scholars about the limiting impact self-interest has as a defining motivation. My strategy colleagues at London Business School, Sumantra Ghoshal and Peter Moran, wrote a seminal piece in which they argued powerfully against the straitjacket that traditional economic theories have placed on our understanding of the world of work and specifically the world of cooperation.[8] Scholars in the field of strategy, which examines cooperation at the level of the company (rather than the individual of psychology or the group of sociology), have written extensively about collaboration and cooperation. A particular interest has been in the evolution of companies from hierarchies to networks.[9] As companies morph into divisional and networked forms, there has also been growing interest in learning how knowledge can be shared across boundaries.

Human resources

There has also been much interest in the organizational practices and processes that create a context in which cooperation and collaboration are more likely to emerge. Strategists such as Katherine Eisenhardt at have used the concept of "dynamic capabilities" to describe how bundles of practices and processes can become crucial as the environment changes and becomes more competitive.[10] The field of human resources has also been concerned with this question. In particular, scholars such as Edward Lawler and Jeffrey Pfeffer have examined the impact of individual reward systems and practices on the likelihood of people cooperating with each other.[11]

Organizational development

Cooperation has been the focus of much interest in the interdisciplinary field of organizational development. Researchers and practicing managers are particularly interested in learning how knowledge is created and sustained within organizations and how organizations change and transform. Michael Polanyi's seminal work on "tacit" and "explicit" knowledge showed that some knowledge was held by the individual while other knowledge was shared within the community.[12] Over the past decade, attention has been devoted to the evolution of "communities of practice" and "communities of creativity." Etienne Wenger's book on communities of practice provided important insights into the phenomenon.[13]

Philosophy

Finally, some of the most incisive questions about cooperation have been asked by philosophers. Aristotle spoke and wrote at length about the importance of cooperation in the citizens of civic societies such as Athens. He believed cooperation to be what he called "natural" in the sense that one's innate striving for excellence would lead one to cooperate with others. My colleagues Janine Nahapiet and Hector Rocha and I have thought long and hard about the impact Aristotle's writing can have on our contemporary view of cooperation.[14] Another ancient philosopher, Socrates, brought insight into our understanding of the nature and development of friendship.[15] Contemporary philosophers are still debating issues around cooperation. I have been particularly influenced by the Oxford philosopher Theodore Zeldin in his thoughts about conversation.[16] In Germany, there remains a strong tradition of philosophy and cooperation, particularly with regard to commitments and action taking.

C

METHODOLOGY OF THE HOT SPOTS RESEARCH

THE RESEARCH FOUNDATION of Hot Spots was established over three stages. The first stage was the creation of an understanding of the body of work on the topic. This literature review is summarized in Appendix B. The second stage was to build a a deeper understanding of Hot Spots by developing case studies of a number of high-performing companies. The final stage was to embark on the Cooperative Advantage Research in collaboration with executives and teams from seventeen companies.

The Case Studies

Our intention in this stage was to get as clear an understanding as possible to what happens when people cooperate, which we pursued through a series of case studies about cooperation. With the exception of the description of Linux, which was drawn from public sources, all the examples of Hot Spots in this book are drawn from these case studies. Each case was developed by interviewing between twenty and thirty people about the company and then identifing a couple of potential Hot Spots and looking at them in more detail. These cases provided an unprecedented insight into the excitement and passion aroused in Hot Spots.

❂ The Cooperative Advantage Research

The final stage of this project was the Cooperative Advantage Research, which involved fifty-seven groups from seventeen companies. These groups were studied using a number of surveys. The first survey asked employees in formal work groups to comment on the context in which they worked, the organizational practices and processes to which they were subject, and their experiences of working cooperatively in the formal work group. The second survey asked many of the same questions, but this time of employees engaged in project teams or task forces. Both surveys asked people to comment on the communities of practice they were engaged in. The third survey was specifically designed for members of the human resource function of the company. The interest here was in the organizational practices and processes the company had in place that could potentially help or hinder cooperation. The fourth and final survey was addressed to the senior executives of the business unit. This survey was designed to tap into the executives' experience of the business environment in which the group operated, their perceptions of the cooperation in the group, and their assessment of the group's performance and outcomes. Here we were particularly interested in the innovation that occurred as a result of the efforts of the group. The major factors explored in those five surveys are shown graphically on the following page.

Cooperation Enablers or Barriers

I. CONTEXTUAL FACTORS

People, Practices, and Processes
- Staffing and promotion
- Socializing
- Network-building human-resource practices
- Training
- Reward systems
- Mentoring

Company Attitude Toward Cooperation
- Values and mission statements
- Conversation
- Human and social capital

Individual Characteristics
- Demographic diversity
- Cultural diversity
- Social identity
- Boundary spanning
- Knowledge and cognition
- Self-monitoring

Technology

Forms of Cooperation

II. FORMS OF COOPERATION
- Work groups
- Task forces
- Project teams
- Communities of practice

Defined by

III. DIMENSIONS OF COOPERATION

The Task Itself
- Purpose of the task
- Commitment to the task
- Proximity
- Boundary-spanning activity

Work on the Task
- Cooperative or competitive goals
- Shared values
- Trust
- Knowledge sharing
- Leadership
- Improvisation

Cooperation versus Competition

IV. COOPERATION vs. COMPETITION
- Productive cooperative behavior
- Unproductive cooperative behavior
- Destructive competitive behavior
- Stimulating competitive behavior

Outcome of Cooperation
- Innovation
- Intrafirm learning
- Overall performance

Notes

Introduction

1. The concept of flow has been regarded as a phenomena that occurs to individuals; See, for example, M. Csikszentmihalyi, *Finding Flow: The Psychology of Engagement with Everyday Life* (New York: Basic Books, 1997). Here I am referring to flow as an individual phenomenon that may also at times happen *between* people.

2. This is an aspect of Hot Spots to which we will return. The scholars in the positive psychology movement have described how high-quality relationships can have a positive and profound effect on our health and well-being; see J. E. Dutton and E. D. Heaphy, "The Power of High-Quality Connections," in K. S. Cameron, J. E. Dutton, and R. E. Quinn (eds.), *Positive Organizational Scholarship: Foundations of a New Discipline* (San Francisco: Berrett-Koehler, 2003). A number of economists have come to the same conclusion. Robert Lane has made the case forcibly in *The Loss of Happiness in Market Democracies* (New Haven, Conn.: Yale University Press, 2000). He reports that friendships and relationships are more positively related to well-being than material wealth. The MORI study on employee engagement shows that employees rate their relationships at work as one of the top five reasons for staying with a company.

3. Issues in cross-functional working have been widely discussed. I have written about the challenges of integrating across functional, business, and geographic boundaries in S. Ghoshal and L. Gratton, "Integrating the Enterprise," *Sloan Management Review* 44 (2002): 31–38.

Chapter 2

1. The argument about the creation of value through combination has been made in some detail by Janine Nahapiet and Sumantra Ghoshal in "Social Capital, Intellectual Capital, and the Organizational Advantage," *Academy of Management Review* 23 (1998): 242–266.

2. This story is drawn from the case "BP: Organizational Transformation," which I prepared with Sumantra Ghoshal and Michelle

Rogan, based on interviews with more than thirty BP executives and employees and examination of a number of documents and financial reports.

3. In a 2005 report by the Economist Intelligence Unit, "KnowHow: Managing Knowledge for Competitive Advantage," 50 percent of the senior executives surveyed reported that "internal barriers to the cross-departmental sharing of information and knowledge" was the main obstacle to achieving the efficient flow and use of knowledge within the organization.

4. This story is drawn from the case "Nokia: The Challenge of Continous Renewal," which I prepared with Sumantra Ghoshal and Alison Donaldson, based on interviews with more than thirty Nokia executives and employees and examination of a number of documents and financial reports.

5. For an overview of the Finnish values of cooperation, see, for example, G. H. Hofstede, *Culture's Consequences: International Differences in Work-Related Values* (Thousand Oaks, Calif.: Sage, 1980).

6. This story is drawn from the case "OgilvyOne: Transformation," which I prepared with Sumantra Ghoshal and Michelle Rogan, based on interviews with more than thirty OgilvyOne executives and employees and examination of a number of documents and financial reports.

7. K. Cheng and D. Gianatasio, "A Look at the Industry Leaders," *Adweek* Midwest Edition. Vol. 40, Issue 42 (1999), p. 82.

8. Estimates of the number of volunteers working on Linux at any given moment range from four thousand to ten thousand. Active developers include around 120 module maintainers, 2,600 patch contributors, and 1,562 debuggers. Jae Yun Moon, "Essence of Distributed Work: The Case of the Linux Kernel," *First Monday,* November 1, 2000, p. 3.

9. For a description of the Linux philosophy and architecture, see P. Evans and B. Wolf, "Collaboration Rules," *Harvard Business Review,* July–August 2005, pp. 96–104, and P. Ghemawat, B. Subirana, and C. B. Pham, "Linux in 2004," Harvard Business School Case 9-705-407.

10. This analysis of DEC was taken from conversations with Sumantra Ghoshal and formed the basis of an article we were preparing when he passed away. In their book *DEC Is Dead, Long Live DEC* (San Francisco: Berrett-Koehler, 2003), Edgar Schein, Peter DeLisi, Paul Kampas, and Michael Sonduck make a similar argument.

Chapter 3

1. The concept of unwritten corporate rules is described in P. Scott Morgan, *The Unwritten Rules of the Game* (New York: McGraw-Hill, 1994).

2. F. Ferraro, J. Pfeffer, and R. Sutton, "Economics Language and Assumptions: How Theories Can Become Self-Fulfilling," *Academy of Management Review* 30 (2005): 8–24.

3. Quoted in N. A. Berg and N. D. Fast, "The Lincoln Electric Company," Harvard Business School Case 376-038.

4. Studies have shown that new hires are socialized into most companies in a remarkably short period of time. For an overview of the development of culture, see E. H. Schein, *Organizational Culture and Leadership* (San Francisco: Jossey-Bass, 1985), and for the impact of culture on firm performance, see J. B. Barney, "Organizational Culture: Can It Be a Source of Sustained Competitive Advantage?" *Academy of Management Review* 11 (1986): 656–665.

5. There is much evidence that our understanding of a company is triggered by language. This language triggers the mental imagery and cognitive schemes that drive our understanding and behavior. For an overview of this, see A. Klamer, D. N. McCloskey, and R. M. Solow (eds.), *The Consequences of Economic Rhetoric* (New York: Cambridge University Press, 1988). As C. W. Mills argues, "We influence a man by naming his acts or imputing motives to them." C. W. Mills, "Situated Actions and the Vocabulary of Motive," *American Sociological Review* 5 (1940): 904–913.

6. V. Liberman, S. Samuels, and L. Ross, "The Name of the Game: Predictive Power of Reputation vs. Situational Labels in Determining Prisoner's Dilemma Game Moves," unpublished manuscript, Department of Psychology, Stanford University, 2003.

7. The incentivization of cooperation is a double-edged sword. Studies into cooperation, for example, have shown that students who are paid to cooperate on a task generally report diminished feelings of self-worth and enjoy the task less than those who have volunteered to perform the task.

8. See O. E. Williamson, *Markets and Hierarchies: Analysis and Antitrust Implications* (New York: Free Press, 1975).

9. A. Smith, *The Wealth of Nations*, ed. E. Cannan (New York: Modern Library, 1994), p. 148 (originally published 1776).

10. Evans and Wolf, "Collaboration Rules."

11. Much of this cycle has been informed by my conversations with Janine Nahapiet and Hector Rocha. Our interest was specifically in how the wisdom of Aristotle could inform our thinking about cooperation. See J. Nahapiet, L. Gratton, and H. Rocha, "Knowledge and Cooperative Relationships: When Cooperation Is the Norm," *European Management Review* 2 (2005): 3–14. In thinking through this cycle, I have also been informed by my colleagues Sumantra Ghoshal and Peter Moran's "Bad for Practice: A Critique of the Transaction Cost Theory," *Academy of Management Review* 21 (1996): 31–47.

12. This is described in S. Broadie, "Philosophical Introduction," in S. Broadie and C. Rowe, *Aristotle: Nicomachean Ethics* (Oxford: Oxford University Press, 2002), pp. 9–91. The notion of striving for excellence or self-efficacy is crucial to the thinking of psychologists such as S. H. Appelbaum and A. Hare, "Self-efficacy as a Mediator of Goal Setting and Performance: Some Human Resource Implications," *Journal of Managerial Psychology* 11 (1966): 33–47.

13. Observations and quotes regarding Goldman Sachs are drawn from the report "Preventing the Death March Towards Mediocrity," which I prepared with Susan Hill and Sumantra Ghoshal, based on interviews with more than thirty of the bank's executives and employees.

14. A thorough review of this topic is provided by A. Kohn, "Why Incentive Plans Cannot Work," *Harvard Business Review,* September–October 1993, pp. 54–69. See also A. Kohn, *Punished by Rewards* (New York: Houghton Mifflin, 1993).

15. This important aspect of cooperation is described in R. Wuthnow, *Acts of Compassion: Caring for Others and Helping Others* (Princeton, N.J.: Princeton University Press, 1991).

16. See B. Uzzi, "The Sources and Consequences of Embeddedness for the Economic Performance of Organizations: The Network Effect," *American Sociological Review* 61 (1996): 674–698, and B. Uzzi, "Social Structure and Competition in Interfirm Networks: The Paradox of Embeddedness," *Administrative Science Quarterly* 42 (1997): 35–67.

17. That high-quality relationships are a conduit for business to be done is the starting assumption of P. Adler and S. W. Kwon, "Social Capital: Prospects for a New Concept," *Academy of Management Review* 27 (2002): 17–40, and is described in depth in R. Cross and P. Parker, *The Hidden Power of Social Networks: Understanding How Work Really Gets Done in Organizations* (Boston: Harvard Business School Press, 2004).

The point is also forcibly made in Dutton and Heaphy, "The Power of High-Quality Connections."

18. Nahapiet and Ghoshal, "Social Capital." A detailed description of the measurement of trust is presented in J. K. Butler Jr., "Toward Understanding and Measuring Conditions of Trust: Evolutions of Conditions of Trust Inventory," *Journal of Management* 17 (1991): 643–663. One of the seminal works on trust is F. Fukuyama, *Trust: Social Virtues and the Creation of Prosperity* (New York: Free Press, 1995).

Chapter 4

1. The distinction between types of knowledge is explored and discussed in M. Polanyi, *The Tacit Dimension* (Garden City, N.Y.: Doubleday, 1996); J. S. Brown and P. Duguid, *The Social Life of Information* (Boston: Harvard Business School Press, 2000); and W. H. Starbuck, "Learning by Knowledge-Intensive Firms," *Journal of Management Studies* 29 (1992): 713–740.

2. See R. S. Burt, *Structural Holes: The Social Structure of Competition* (Cambridge, Mass.: Harvard University Press, 1992), and D. Krackhardt, "The Strength of Strong Ties: The Importance of Philos in Organizations," in N. Nohria and R. G. Eccles (eds.), *Networks and Organizations* (Boston: Harvard Business School Press, 1992), pp. 216–239.

3. See ibid.; R. S. Burt, "'The Network Structure of Social Capital," *Research in Organizational Behavior* 22 (2000): 345–423; M. Granovetter, "The Strength of Weak Ties," *American Journal of Sociology* 78 (1973): 1360–1380; M. T. Hansen, "The Search-Transfer Problem: The Role of Weak Ties in Sharing Knowledge Across Organizational Subunits," *Administrative Science Quarterly* 44 (1999): 82–111; G. Szulanski, "Exploring Internal Stickiness: Impediments to the Transfer of Best Practice Within the Firm," *Strategic Management Journal* 17 (1996): 27–43; and Uzzi, "Social Structure and Competition." Cross and Parker's *The Hidden Power of Social Networks* describes how these networks can be plotted and understood. For a more concise description, see R. Cross, S. P. Borgatti, and A. Parker, "Making Invisible Work Visible: Using Social Network Analysis to Support Strategic Collaboration," *California Management Review* 22 (2002): 25–46, and for a managerial perspective, see W. Baker, *Achieving Success Through Social Capital: Tapping the Hidden Resources in Your Personal and Business Networks* (San Francisco: Jossey-Bass, 2000).

4. For a description of the benefits of autonomous business units and the challenges associated with them, see S. Ghoshal and L. Gratton, "Integrating the Enterprise," *Sloan Management Review* 44 (2002): 31–38. For a rich description and analysis of tension in the context of large, divisionalized companies, see C. K. Prahalad and Y. L. Doz, *The Multinational Mission: Balancing Local Demands and Global Vision* (New York: Free Press, 1987).

5. See J. Lave and E. C. Wenger, *Situated Learning: Legitimate Peripheral Participation* (New York: Cambridge University Press, 1991); E. C. Wenger, R. McDermott, and W. M. Snyder, *Communities of Practice: A Guide to Managing Knowledge* (Boston: Harvard Business School Press, 2002); and Brown and Duguid, *Social Life of Information.*

6. P. Ghemawat, B. Subirana, and C. B. Pham, "Linux in 2004," Harvard Business School Case 9-705-407.

7. See J. Lipnack and J. Stamps, *The Age of the Network: Organizing Principles of the 21st Century* (New York: Wiley, 1994). The research on proximity began at MIT in the late 1970s. See T. J. Allen, *Managing the Flow of Technology: Technology Transfer and the Dissemination of Technology Information Within the R&D Organization* (Cambridge, Mass.: MIT Press, 1977).

8. It has been found that on a wide range of demographic characteristics (such as age, education, race, religion, and socioeconomic status), people who go together (friends, dates, spouses) resemble each other; see B. L. Warren, "A Multiple Variable Approach to the Assortive Mating Phenomenon," *Eugenics Quarterly* 13 (1966): 285–298. The same is true regarding physical attractiveness and attraction and regarding attitudes and attraction; see A. Feingold, "Matching for Attractiveness in Romantic Partners and Same-Sex Friends: A Meta-Analysis and Theoretical Critique," *Psychological Bulletin* 104 (1988): 226–235, and D. Byrne, et al., "The Ubiquitous Relationship: Attitude Similarity and Attraction: A Cross-Cultural Study," *Human Relations* 24 (1971): 201–207.

9. This point about collectivism was made by G. H. Hofstede in *Culture's Consequences: International Differences in Work-Related Values* (Thousand Oaks, Calif.: Sage, 1980). Later studies argued that the collectivistic nature of Asian cultures makes the notion of self-interest harder to comprehend; see H. R. Markus and S. Kitayama, "Culture and the Self: Implications for Cognition, Emotion, and Motivation," *Psychological Review* 98 (1991): 224–253.

10. See L. Gratton, *Living Strategy: Putting People at the Heart of Corporate Purpose* (London: Financial Times/Prentice Hall, 2002).

11. See M. Waller, J. Conte, C. Gibson, and M. Carpenter, "The Effect of Individual Perceptions of Deadlines on Team Performance," *Academy of Management Review* 26 (2001): 586–600.

12. For more on this point, see D. E. Vinton, "A New Look at Time, Speed, and the Manager," *Academy of Management Executive* 6 (1992): 7–16.

13. See M. J. Waller, R. C. Giambatista, and M. Zellmer-Bruhn, "The Effect of Individual Time Differences on Group Polychronicity," *Journal of Managerial Psychology* 13 (1999): 244–256.

14. E. J. Johnson, J. W. Payne, and J. R. Bettman, "Adapting to Time Constraints," in O. Svenson and A. J. Maule (eds.), *Time Pressure and Stress in Human Judgment and Decision Making* (New York: Plenum, 1993), pp. 103–116.

15. T. Hall, *The Dance of Time: The Other Dimension of Time* (Garden City, N.Y.: Anchor/Doubleday, 1983).

16. As time goes on, in-group members evaluate themselves more positively and rate members of out-groups more negatively by projecting negative stereotypes and prejudices onto them; see F. J. Flynn, J. A. Chatman, and S. E. Spataro, "Getting to Know You: The Influence of Personality on Impressions and Performance of Demographically Different People in Organizations," *Administrative Science Quarterly* 46 (2001): 414–442.

17. Stereotyping occurs as members with a common identity characterize others whom they perceive to be different. According to the *Random House* unabridged dictionary, a stereotype is "a simplified and standardized conception or image invested with special meaning and held in common by members of a group." Consequently, human beings have a certain preference for interacting with people who exhibit similar sociodemographic characteristics, behaviors, and personalities; see M. McPherson, L. Smith-Lovin, and J. M. Cook, "Birds of a Feather: Homophily in Social Networks," *Annual Review of Sociology,* 27 (2001): 415–444; H. Tajfel, *Social Identity and Intergroup Behavior* (New York: Cambridge University Press, 1982); and H. Tajfel, M. Billig, R. Bundy, and C. Flament, "Social Categorization and Intergroup Behavior," *European Journal of Social Psychology,* 1 (1971): 149–178.

18. "Playful exchanges" is a phrase from R. Oldenburg, *The Great Good Place* (New York: Paragon House, 1991).

19. M. Kilduff and W. Tsai, *Social Networks and Organizations* (Thousand Oaks, Calif.: Sage, 2003).

20. See C. P. Alderfer, "Boundary Relations and Organizational Diagnosis," in M. Meltzer and F. Wickert (eds.), *Humanizing Organizational Behavior* (Springfield, Ill.: Thomas, 1976), pp. 142–175, and D. G. Ancona and D. Caldwell, "Bridging the Boundary: External Activity and Performance in Organizational Teams," *Administrative Science Quarterly* 37 (1992): 634–665.

21. Burt, *Structural Holes;* Burt, "Network Structure of Social Capital."

22. See R. T. Keller, "Cross-Functional Project Groups in Research and New Product Development: Diversity, Communications, Job Stress, and Outcomes," *Academy of Management Journal* 44 (2001): 547–555.

23. See Granovetter, "The Strength of Weak Ties."

24. For a more complete description of Nokia's network structure, see L. Gratton, "Managing Integration Through Cooperation," *Human Resource Management,* 44 (2005): 151–158.

25. G. H. Hofstede, *Culture's Consequences: International Differences in Work-Related Values* (Thousand Oaks, Calif.: Sage, 1980)

Chapter 5

1. C. A. Kenwood, "A Business Case Study of Open Source Software," MITRE Corp., July 2001, <http://www.mitre.org/work/tech_papers/tech_papers_01/kenwood_software/kenwood_software.pdf>, p. 13.

2. "Wikipedia Founder Jimmy Wales Responds," Slashdot, July 28, 2004, <http://interviews.slashdot.org/article.pl?sid=04/07/28/1351230>.

3. See D. Whyte, *The Heart Aroused: Poetry and Preservation of the Soul of Corporate America* (New York: Currency/Doubleday, 1994).

4. The impact of conversation on purpose is explained in L. Gratton and S. Ghoshal, "Improving the Quality of Conversations," *Organizational Dynamics* 31 (2002): 209–223. There are many interesting articles and books on purposeful conversation. I have benefited particularly from T. Zeldin, *Conversation: How Talk Can Change Your Life* (London: Harvill Press, 1998), and D. Bohm, *On Dialogue* (New York: Routledge, 1996). An overview of more rational conversation is provided in K. van der Heijden, *Scenarios: The Art of Strategic Conversation* (New York: Free Press, 1996). B. Isaac, "Taking Flight: Dialogue, Collective Thinking, and Organizational Learning," *Organizational Dynamics* 1 (1999): 24–39, provides a useful conceptual framework, and C. Hardy, T. B. Lawrence, and N. Phillips, "Talk and Action: Conversations and Narratives in

Interorganizational Collaboration, in D. Grant, T. W. Keenoy, and C. Oswick (eds.), *Discourse and Organization* (Thousand Oaks, Calif.: Sage, 1998), pp. 65–82, present a convincing argument on the impact on collaboration.

5. *Economist* survey of new media, April 22, 2006, pp 26–35.

6. Zeldin, *Conversation*, p. 14.

7. G. Egan, *You and Me: The Skills of Communicating and Relating to Each Other* (Belmont, Calif.: Wadsworth, 1977).

8. L. L. Putnam, N. Philips, and P. Chapman, "Metaphors of Communication and Organization," in S. R. Clegg, C. Hardy, and W. R. Nords (eds.), *Handbook of Organizational Studies* (Thousand Oaks, Calif.: Sage, 1996), p. 391.

9. See K. E. Weick, "Improvisation as a Mindset for Organizational Analysis," *Organizational Studies* 9 (1998): 543–555.

10. L. Gratton, *The Democratic Enterprise* (London: Financial Times/ Prentice Hall, 2004).

11. There is much evidence that successful CEOs have well-established networks both inside and outside the company. See, for example, R. Boyatzi and A. McKee, *The Resonant Leader* (Boston: Harvard Business School Press, 2006).

12. Csikszentmihalyi, M. *Flow: The Psychology of Optimal Experience* (New York: HarperCollins, 1990).

Chapter 6

1. D. N. Sull and C. Spinosa, 'Using Commitments to Manage Across Units," *MIT Sloan Management Review* 47 (2005): 73–81.

2. See C. Nemeth, "Minority Dissent and Its 'Hidden Benefits,'" *New Review of Social Psychology* 2 (2003): 21–28.

3. R. Pascale, *Managing on the Edge* (New York: Simon & Schuster, 1990); see also R. Pascale, M. Millemann, and L. Gioja, *Surfing at the Edge of Chaos: The Laws of Nature and the New Laws of Business* (London: Texere, 2000).

4. For a useful overview of the impact of time on groups, see J. E. McGrath, "Time Matters in Groups," in R. E. Kraut, J. R. Galegher, and C. Egido (eds.), *Intellectual Teamwork* (Hillsdale, N.J.: Erlbaum, 1990), pp. 23–61.

5. D. G. Ancona and C. L. Chong, "Entrainment: Pace, Cycle, and Rhythm in Organizational Behavior," *Research in Organizational Behavior* 18 (1996): 251–284.

6. See S. Blount and G. Janicik, "When Plans Change: Examining How People Evaluate Timing Changes in Work Organizations," *Academy of Management Review,* 26 (2001): 566–585.

7. D. G. Ancona, P. S. Goodman, B. S. Lawrence, and M. L. Tushman, "Time: A New Research Lens," *Academy of Management Review* 26 (2001): 654–663.

8. See M. C. Moore-Ede, F. M. Sulzman, and C. A. Fuller, *The Clocks That Time Us* (Cambridge, Mass.: Harvard University Press, 1982).

9. P. R. Carlile, "A Pragmatic View of Knowledge and Boundaries: Boundary Objects in New Product Development," *Organizational Science* 13 (2002): 442–455.

10. D. G. Ancona and C. L. Chong, "Entrainment: Pace, Cycle, and Rhythm in Organizational Behavior," *Research in Organizational Behavior* 18 (1996): 251–284.

11. B. W. Hesse, C. M. Werner, and I. Altman, *Temporal Aspects of Computer-Mediated Communications* (Salt Lake City: University of Utah, 1987).

12. E. Jacques, *The Form of Time* (New York: Crane Russak, 1982).

13. C. Mainemelis, "When the Muse Takes It All: A Model for the Experience of Timelessness in Organizations," *Academy of Management Review* 26 (2001): 548–565.

14. Ibid. See also E. L. Deci and R. M. Ryan, *Intrinsic Motivation and Self-Determination in Human Behavior* (New York: Plenum, 1985).

15. L. A. Perlow, "The Time Famine: Toward a Sociology of Work Time," *Administrative Science Quarterly* 44 (1999): 57–81.

16. R. M. Ryan and E. L. Deci, "Self-Determination Theory and the Facilitation of Intrinsic Motivation, Social Development, and Well-Being," *American Psychologist* 55 (2000): 66–78.

17. H. Gardner, *Multiple Intelligences: The Theory in Practice* (New York: Basic Books, 1993).

Appendix B

1. A. Maslow, *The Farthest Reaches of Human Nature* (New York: Viking, 1971)

2. See R. Hackman, "The Design of Work Teams," in J. W. Lorsch (ed.), *Handbook of Organizational Behavior* (Englewood cliffs, N.J.: Prentice Hall, 1987).

3. R. Putnam, *Making Democracy Work: Civic Traditions in Modern Italy* (Princeton, N.J.: Princeton University Press, 1993).

4. The measurement of ties is still a very hot topic, and research continues in the field; see Burt, *Structural Holes.* Companies have applied network analysis to understand the extent of social ties and their impact on social capital; see Baker, *Achieving Success Through Social Capital.*

5. See Burt, *Structural Holes* and "Network Structure of Social Capital" and Granovetter, "Strength of Weak Ties"; see also M. T. Hansen, "'The Search-Transfer Problem: The Role of Weak Ties in Sharing Knowledge Across Organizational Subunits," *Administrative Science Quarterly* 44 (1999): 82–111.

6. See, for example, R. Axelrod, *The Evolution of Cooperation* (New York: Basic Books, 1984).

7. See, for example, A. K. Sen, "Rational Fools: A Critique of the Behavioral Foundations of Economic Theory," in J. J. Mansbridge (ed.), *Beyond Self-Interest* (Chicago: University of Chicago Press, 1990), pp. 25–43.

8. Ghoshal and Moran, "Bad for Practice."

9. See, for example, N. Nohria and S. Ghoshal, *The Differentiated Network* (Boston: Harvard Business School Press, 1997).

10. See, for example, S. L. Brown and K. M. Eisenhardt, *Competing on the Edge: Strategy as Structured Chaos* (Boston: Harvard Business School Press, 1998).

11. See, for example, E.E. Lawler, *Treating People Right: How organizations and individuals can propel each other into a virtuous spiral of success* (San Francisco: Jossey Bass, 2003), and J. Pfeffer and C. Reilly, *Hidden Value: how great companies achieve extraordinary results with ordinary people.*(Boston: Harvard Business School Press, 2000).

12. Polanyi, *The Tacit Dimension.*

13. E. C. Wenger, *Communities of Practice: Learning, Meaning, and Identity* (New York: Cambridge University Press, 1998); E. C. Wenger and W. M. Snyder, "Communities of Practice: The Organizational Frontier," *Harvard Business Review,* January–February 2000, pp. 139–145.

14. See Nahapiet et al., "Knowledge and Cooperative Relationships."

15. Since none of what Socrates wrote remains today, the accounts of his teaching and life are all secondhand in Xenophon, Aristophanes, Aristotle, and—chiefly—Plato.

16. T. Zeldin, *Conversation.*

Index

About the Author

L YNDA GRATTON is professor of management practice at London Business School, where she directs the school's executive program, Human Resource Strategy in Transforming Organisations. Over the past two decades, Gratton has led two major research consortiums linking academics with executives. The first, launched in 1995, was the Leading Edge Research Consortium (http://www.london.edu/lerc), a major research initiative involving companies such as Hewlett-Packard and Citibank. The initial results from the research were published by Oxford University Press in 2000 in the book *Strategic Human Resource Management: Corporate Rhetoric and Human Reality*. In 2005, Gratton launched a second research consortium, the Cooperative Research Initiative, supported by companies such as the BBC, Reuters, and Nokia.

In *Living Strategy: Putting People at the Heart of Corporate Purpose*, published by Financial Times/Prentice Hall in 2000, Gratton called for a more strategic approach to people management. The book has been translated into a dozen languages and was voted one of the twenty most influential books on management by American CEOs. More recently, she has addressed the issue of organizational purpose in *The Democratic Enterprise: Liberating Your Business with Freedom, Flexibility, and Commitment,* published by Financial Times/Prentice Hall in 2004.

Gratton has written for managers and academics. Her article "Integrating the Enterprise" was named the *Sloan Management Review*'s best article of 2003, and her case on BP was recently proclaimed the best overall case of 2006 by ecch (formerly the European Case Clearing House).

In 2005, Gratton was named by the *London Times* as one of the top fifty thinkers in the world. She is acknowledged as one of the world's most accomplished masters of HR strategy and was in 2006 ranked in the top ten of *Human Resources Magazine*'s Top 100 Most Influential poll. In 2004, Gratton was appointed senior fellow of the Advanced Institute of Management in the United Kingdom (http://www.aim-research.org) and in 2006 as director of the Lehman Centre for Women in Business.

Gratton lives in London and Sitges, Spain, with her two sons. Her Web site can be visited at http://www.lyndagratton.com.

About Berrett-Koehler Publishers

Berrett-Koehler is an independent publisher dedicated to an ambitious mission: Creating a World that Works for All.

We believe that to truly create a better world, action is needed at all levels—individual, organizational, and societal. At the individual level, our publications help people align their lives and work with their deepest values. At the organizational level, our publications promote progressive leadership and management practices, socially responsible approaches to business, and humane and effective organizations. At the societal level, our publications advance social and economic justice, shared prosperity, sustainable development, and new solutions to national and global issues.

We publish groundbreaking books focused on each of these levels. To further advance our commitment to positive change at the societal level, we have recently expanded our line of books in this area and are calling this expanded line "BK Currents."

A major theme of our publications is "Opening Up New Space." They challenge conventional thinking, introduce new points of view, and offer new alternatives for change. Their common quest is changing the underlying beliefs, mindsets, institutions, and structures that keep generating the same cycles of problems, no matter who our leaders are or what improvement programs we adopt.

We strive to practice what we preach—to operate our publishing company in line with the ideas in our books. At the core of our approach is *stewardship*, which we define as a deep sense of responsibility to administer the company for the benefit of all of our "stakeholder" groups: authors, customers, employees, investors, service providers, and the communities and environment around us. We seek to establish a partnering relationship with each stakeholder that is open, equitable, and collaborative.

We are gratified that thousands of readers, authors, and other friends of the company consider themselves to be part of the "BK Community." We hope that you, too, will join our community and connect with us through the ways described on our website at www.bkconnection.com.

BE CONNECTED

Visit Our Website

Go to www.bkconnection.com to read exclusive previews and excerpts of new books, find detailed information on all Berrett-Koehler titles and authors, browse subject-area libraries of books, and get special discounts.

Subscribe to Our Free E-Newsletter

Be the first to hear about new publications, special discount offers, exclusive articles, news about bestsellers, and more! Get on the list for our free e-newsletter by going to www.bkconnection.com.

Participate in the Discussion

To see what others are saying about our books and post your own thoughts, check out our blogs at www.bkblogs.com.

Get Quantity Discounts

Berrett-Koehler books are available at quantity discounts for orders of ten or more copies. Please call us toll-free at (800) 929-2929 or e-mail us at bkp.orders@aidcvt.com.

Host a Reading Group

For tips on how to form and carry on a book reading group in your workplace or community, see our website at www.bkconnection.com.

Join the BK Community

Thousands of readers of our books have become part of the "BK Community" by participating in events featuring our authors, reviewing draft manuscripts of forthcoming books, spreading the word about their favorite books, and supporting our publishing program in other ways. If you would like to join the BK Community, please contact us at bkcommunity@bkpub.com.